The BEATING of GREAT WINGS

**A Worldly Spirituality
for Active, Apostolic Communities**

BERNARD J. LEE, S.M.

The BEATING of GREAT WINGS

**A Worldly Spirituality
for Active, Apostolic Communities**

TWENTY-THIRD PUBLICATIONS

185 WILLOW STREET • PO BOX 180 • MYSTIC, CT 06355
TEL: 1-800-321-0411 • FAX: 1-800-572-0788
Bayard   E-MAIL: ttpubs@aol.com • www.twentythirdpublications.com

The Scripture passages contained herein are from the *New Revised Standard Version of the Bible*, copyright ©1989, by the Division of Christian Education of the National Council of Churches in the U.S.A. All rights reserved.

Cover illustration by Steve Ersparmer.

Twenty-Third Publications
A Division of Bayard
185 Willow Street
P.O. Box 180
Mystic, CT 06355
(860) 536-2611 or (800) 321-0411
www.twentythirdpublications.com
ISBN:1-58595-310-5

Library of Congress Catalog Card Number: 20031133304
Printed in the USA.

Epigraph

We must be broken because there is a good so great
it breaks the bounds of our littleness.

We must be broken because there is a power
which works in our lives to achieve a good
we cannot compass and cannot discern,
until some later time in retrospect,
reveals the form of a new creation
now visibly emerging.

We must be broken because there is a God
who works for righteousness so great
that it cannot be confined to the limits of our control.

We must be broken because there is, day by day,
the creating of a kingdom of goodness
in depth and height and scope
so far beyond the reach of any human plan
that it must not be constricted to our imposed directive.

We must be broken because above us,
above the breakdown and the ruin
of plans and persons and ages and nations,
there is a beating of great wings.

—Henry Nelson Wieman, *The Source of Human Good*

CONTENTS

ONE

BROKEN AND BUILDING

Introduction

Simply and clearly, this is not a systematic theology or spirituality or history of religious life. It is a collection of meditations that have been building. They are the product of experience and of many conversations with others, over many years. I do not speak on behalf of my conversation partners. And I do not offer my reflections as the product of the inexorable logic of experience. They are just meditations, although they do venture into practical theology.

Broken and Building

We in religious life in the United States are being broken because we must be broken. And we are part of a church that is being broken. That is why I chose the words of Henry Nelson Wieman for the epigraph. In 1965 we religious numbered 216,000. Today our number is down to 106,000, and only 3.5 percent of us are under the age of forty. We are often afraid. And sometimes this makes us bold.

We ask the Holy Spirit to remake the face of the earth, seldom comprehending the breaking that remaking requires. It is painful. We know the right phrases. "Asceticism" means cutting and pruning. And "a grain of wheat must first fall to the ground and die if it is to produce more grain." I hear us evoke often enough the rhetoric of hope. I do it also, but not readily with the openness to being reshaped, reconstructed, revamped, refurbished—remade, top to bottom, inside and out—in a word, broken. Yet if we listen together very quietly, I wager we can hear, albeit so faintly, the beating of great wings.

I want to say at the outset that this book is not about recovering religious life, or renewing religious life, but rebuilding it or perhaps even reinventing it, by setting it upon different, non-traditional foundational stones.

The death of God movement in the 1960s borrowed a lot of its vocabulary from Friedrich Nietzsche. What most interpreters of that movement have come to recognize is that what had died was much of the symbolic structure that mediated the experience of God. All experience of God is symbolically mediated. When the world-view in which a symbolic world is anchored undergoes very significant transformation, much of the symbolism loses its effectiveness. And what was mediated by it seems to have been lost. We don't think "the symbolism for God doesn't work"; we think, rather, "where did God go?" A lot of symbolism around transcendence has been impaired, and that is one of the efforts of this book: to recapture the transcendence of God in symbolic structures of historical experience, and to consider how that might functionally affect active, apostolic congregations.

In his book, *Deep Symbols: Their Postmodern Effacement and Reclamation*, Edward Farley writes that "the religious community must never pretend that its own deep symbols float above history in a world of ideal meanings....[For] one feature of deep symbols is their necessary connection with specific peoples and cultures" (pp. 8, 13). While deep symbols do not change easily or quickly, they are very vulnerable to deep historical changes, and a new symbolic structure is not just waiting in the wings to move on stage. The time between disenchantment and re-enchantment is fraught with anxiety, a near-empty stage. It is the experience of being broken that hopes for the beating of great wings. Catholics know that angst well, often without knowing whence it comes.

The reinvention that stirs the great wings to beat involves many composite remakings. The largest of these reinventing foundation stones is probably a change in the relationship between the *vita contemplativa* and the *vita activa*, i.e., taking seriously that action is the normative human condition, and that history is the locus of our experience of God. Action has a more specific meaning than activity, which will be addressed later. For Christians, action (not identical to activity) is the exercised responsibility for collaborating with God historically in the redemption of historical experience.

There is also a counter-cultural position (counter to US culture) that community is the basic social unit, not the individual, whether about the human condition generally, or about the way that God redeems us (redeems "me" because of the "us" to which I and we belong). The recovery of community in US Catholic culture through a recovery of Word and Eucharist as utterly central and radically social is a redemptive thrust for which religious life might lead the way. But to do that, our spiritual practice and exercises must invite sustained scrutiny. The sacramentality of the world belongs to this endeavor.

Religious life, while grounded in gospel values, does not have a specific gospel constitution. Its nature is its history: what we have done, what we are doing, what we shall do. Celibate community-in-mission is a particularly keen insight into our historical nature.

Overview

The reflections that follow are not a comprehensive overview of the history and theology of religious life. I applaud the comprehensiveness and vision of the recent work by Sr. Sandra Schneiders in this regard. My concerns are far more limited and basic. I want to explore the rebuilding of Christian Catholic life with Word and Eucharist utterly at our center. That is everybody's challenge, not just for religious. But it is perhaps true that religious life can mediate this centrality for the life of the Church.

For us in religious life, retrieval efforts will be further shaped by the place of the retrieval—celibate community—and by the regular participation of a religious community's "deep story" in the conversation. I believe further that the vocation of active apostolic communities is far more akin to the vocation of the laity than to clerical life. Being-in-the-world, a world for which God has specified intentions, is our social location. And "active" as I choose to use it is not in contrast with "contemplative," but rather an interpretation of the human condition (a theological anthropology, which will be explored later in this text).

Several themes that I find significantly interconnected shape the materials in this book, very much in the mode and mood of practical theology. A socio-historical theology of charism is the starting point. The two chapters that follow address Word and Eucharist as the essential and central "practices" or "exercises" of a religious community's (or any Catholic's) spirituality. This is no simple task, given the accretions that have accumulated both within religious communities and in Catholic culture more broadly. Biblical scholarship has transformed the dynamics of breaking open the Word, and the recovery of the richness and variety of our understandings and practices of Eucharist has opened and deepened Catholic culture. But none of this is without challenge and travail.

Next is the profound but always critical affection that we must bear towards the world from our only vantage point, which is within the world. World is where mission happens, because world is where God's intentions for history are to be lived. And world is what shapes us more deeply than we know. We are in the world and the world is in us.

Finally, community and vows go together. There is not much that separates the commitments of active, apostolic communities and most of the lay people of God, except that our life is lived in the context of celibate community.

We will then attempt a brief interpretation of the vows. Many of the tasks described above are every Christian's tasks. What defines religious life is that celibate community is the working context for men and women in active apostolic orders who work at the same perfection and at many of the same tasks as all of the people of God. The closing chapter is about community and mission, or better still, about communities-in-permanent-mission. The epilogue concerns the prophetic vocation of religious life.

Here is an initial orientation towards those thematic concerns.

One: Charism and Deep Story

It has been commonplace since the Second Vatican Council for religious orders to see as their task the recovery of our originating charism, with new power in a new time. I understand the intent of those words, but will recommend breaking charism into two components that help clarify the task. One component is a sociological reading of the nature of charism. The other component is an anthropological reading of a community's deep story. Charism cannot be recovered; it can only be reinvented, and that happens when a community's deep story speaks effective, felt words to the transformation of some of the world's most pressing needs and aspirations. A deep story's acute responsiveness to critical, unmet human need gives us our best chance of hearing the beating of great wings.

We like to think of our founders and foundresses as being ahead of their time. That may be part of the rhetoric of hope, but in many ways it is a misreading. The fact is that they are radically [in their roots] people of their time, immersed in their time, responsive to their time. Often their time is the beginning of a new time. That is why the rhetoric of hope comes easy. But they are responding to "what is," sometimes with intuition that the newness in "what is" is a harbinger. Or better yet, they intuit that the world which the Spirit is remaking is, even now, already breaking into the present. Patricia Wittberg (whom I shall cite often in this book) warns against overemphasizing the individual founder or foundress and the supernatural at the expense of the social factors at work. "Societal" is not at odds with "supernatural"; it simply names the historical mediation of God's active presence for those whose energies and efforts got us started. They hear some beating of great wings, but "what is" is the operative matrix, not "what will be." The future is God's secret and God's promise, and it is in the present that we open ourselves to new prospects for God's intentions for the world. This is not a bias against our task of futuring, only an acknowledgment of its limitations because futures from God outstrip predictive gifts.

I believe that hope is the key, and hope is sorely needed as religious see their numbers dwindle and experience uncertainty about their mission. Hope requires imagination about alternatives, a firm belief that things ought to be different. The difference between imagination and hope is that hope is open to God's imagination, but it is our own active imagination that prepares the way. Any present moment can be quite thin, or it can be quite thick. The "what is" of founders and foundresses is very thick: they remember a lot. As Walt Whitman said, we contain multitudes. If much is remembered, just as much is anticipated. We attend to the present, with poignant memory and vivid anticipation on either side. New communities are incubated in the immediacies of profoundly lived, accurately interpreted, and deeply felt experience, filled to the brim with memory and hope.

Also part of the rhetoric of hope is to speak of our founders and foundresses as prophetic. And that too is often misunderstood. Prophets did not presage the future. The prophets, rather, knew the demands of the age to come upon the present moment. In Christian terms, a prophet knows what the initiated but unconsummated Reign of God needs from us right now.

Two: the Enacted Word

Often in the text that follows I will speak of the conversation between the Word and the world, which animated the prophets of old, the founders and foundresses, and will again animate new prophets, new founders and foundresses, and the refounders and refoundresses. By Word I mean the privileged place of Scripture, but also the many resources of faith: tradition, doctrine, liturgy, spirituality, a religious community's experience, and certainly the new Words that God speaks, mediated by the time and place in which we live our lives right now. In this text, "Word" will often be a metaphor for that rich assemblage of faith and its resources, but especially Scripture.

Martin Buber remarks that people sometimes wonder why God no longer speaks to his people. His answer is that we do not hear the new speech of God because we expect it to be uttered either above everyday life or alongside every day life (Buber, 1958, 136-137). But in fact it is when the events in which we are engaged call us to decision that the personal speech of God occurs. Here again, it is at the conflux of Word and world that God's speaking happens. Founders, foundresses, and prophets have caught the vocabulary, grammar, and rhetoric of the historically mediated speech of God.

While I will consider Word a metaphor for all of the resources of faith, the First Word is that of Scripture. Of all the resources of faith that nourish us, Scripture is paramount. Above all, the Word, while it must be heard, is not there for the hearing alone. It is there for enactment. Perhaps, shy of enactment, we should call it true word on the way to most true Word.

In this chapter I will also suggest that the experience of small Christian communities in the US Catholic Church can be a resource for religious communities seeking to give some compelling centrality to the power of God's Word. Besides that, the learning and teaching back and forth would be good for us all. When this comes to pass, quite possibly the flutter of the beating of great wings will grow very loud.

Eucharist

Eucharist is in some ways currently a Catholic minefield. Two issues in particular haunt our contemporary sensibilities. The first is negotiating the tension between a sensualist and a merely symbolist interpretation of real presence. Both sides are grounded in theological reflection that in turn is grounded in philosophical presuppositions, often naively understood.

The second area is the recovering the notion of the assembled community as the liturgical subject, rather than the priest alone as the liturgical subject. Recent documents from Rome concerning Eucharist betray a fear that priestly identity is at stake. What is perhaps at stake is a theology of priestly identity that requires serious new attention. Conscious, full, active participation in liturgy requires some deepening insight into the constitutive relationship between a community and its leader.

While these are everybody's issues, religious communities, precisely because of the lived experience of community life, are in a position, as the saying goes, to push the envelope a bit; or, in different language, to occasion some prophetic verve. Eucharist, like word/Word, is also a community's enactment of its reality as Body of Christ.

Action and Speech in the World

By world I mean all of the social systems, large and small, in which we live, from friendships and family size to world politics and economics, and the ways we interpret all of that. In his recent book on the Christian Sacraments in a Postmodern World, Kenan Osborne characterizes human life as "drenched in temporality." I want to add that we are also drenched in locality. We can never escape our historical and cultural conditioning. We cannot retrieve our founding moment because we cannot retrieve that time or that place. The founding experience in its founding particularity is simply not repeatable because time and place are not repeatable. We can only reinvent charism in a new time and place, by remembering together accurately and selectively who we have been, and by anticipating imaginatively who we might yet be, drenched in new time and new place, and alas with spectacular memory.

One does not have to live long to know that the world's resistance to transformation is deep and abiding, and that the dark side is never too distant. Wieman names that painful reality, but his hope still hears the beating of great wings. Somewhere deep in Catholic faith, as in biblical faith, we are a world-affirming people, because God made the world. This is an expression of what David Tracy calls Catholic culture's "analogical imagination."

The Second Vatican Council, in *Gaudium et Spes*, says that it focuses on the human world, the whole human family along with the sum of those realities in the midst of which that family lives. It gazes upon the world which is the theatre of human history, and carries the marks of our energies, our tragedies, and our triumphs—the world that the Christian sees as created and sustained by its maker's love, fallen indeed into the bondage of sin, yet emancipated now by Christ.

In the economy of redemption God requires human collaboration in the emancipation that comes only through Christ.

In our attention to the world, we will pay particular attention to the acculturation of religious life in American culture of the early twenty-first century. To this end, we will have to negotiate the difficult terrain of theological anthropology as an underpinning of active, apostolic community life.

Community-in-Mission and the Vows

There are multiple dimensions to this topic. Community is the shape of anyone's membership in the body of Christ. Living responsibly within the framework of the world's and the family's and the community's resources is everyone's responsibility, as are "obeying" the common good and living chastely. Religious vows reflect the texture of the celibate community.

Within our culture, in which individualism is so marked, community life and family life are in serious trouble. It may be one of the callings of religious communities to create models that are functional and attractive. The redemption of our modes of togetherness needs "redeemers," those who collaborate with the Christ event in empowering our many layered relational webs.

Charism, word, Eucharist, world, and the celibate community-in-permanent-mission are the topics of this book. There are, of course, many meanings of "community" within celibate life. What I do not mean by community is simply a living arrangement for members of the same religious order, but without a substantial inner life among them, or without the kind of conversation that actively shapes their mission—whether novices or retired religious, or everything in between.

Known Presuppositions

In several recent books, I have begun with some largely autobiographical reflections, not because I think they are inherently interesting, but because a reader deserves to be informed about the biases and presuppositions a writer brings to his work.

First of all, the reflections in this book are something of an exercise in social imagination, a meditation on new ways of understanding experience in new categories in a new time. It is the tradition reshaping itself, as the Church does with its own life: *ecclesia semper reformanda*. This is a critical time for religious life. When the power, insight, and wisdom of Vatican II have more largely taken hold, religious life will have a different look.

Second, while religious life responds generously to gospel values, it does not have a structural gospel warrant. No gospel text links celibacy and community as a form of discipleship, or celibacy and community leadership as internally connected. We have made some rich connections that have shaped Catholic culture inside and out. And we are free to continue imagining because religious life has no nature other that what it has been, is, and yet shall be. That, of course, is really a lot. I believe that this time is a very historically open time.

Third, all of this book's ruminations are in the mode of practical theology: a structured, critical conversation about various interpretations of religious life and interpretations of the social, cultural, and intellectual worlds in which we live right now. The purpose of this practical theological conversation is to generate strategic pastoral agenda for religious life so that it may serve well the Reign of God. This kind of conversation is, to use an image from Latin America, a gathering after the sun goes down to process what happened when the sun was high, and no one retires until tomorrow's agenda gets clarified.

What I find appealing about practical theology is that it has the same form as the structure of Christian experience: listening to God in all the ways that God speaks, listening hard to the concrete realities of our lived experience, and implementing the meanings that arise from the dialogue between them.

Fourth, I am a male and have lived since 1956 in a male religious order. I have taught in two high schools, and have had faculty positions in four universities, three sponsored by men's religious communities, one by a women's religious community. I have helped in parishes but never have had a parish assignment; and I have done retreat work. While I have had extensive interaction with members of women's religious communities, I know that I cannot see the religious life from feminine perspective the way Sandra Schneiders has done in her recent work. Much insightful writing has come from women religious. The Leadership Conference of Women Religious has been bold and articulate and true. I admire religious women's experience exceedingly. They brought the US Catholic Church into the post-conciliar ecclesial world. Yet I know I cannot transcend the limitations of seeing religious life as a man whose principal context has been a male religious order.

Fifth, although I have some experience of religious communities outside of the United States, this country is the social location that I have in mind throughout the book. This is, of course, a formidable limitation. But the US Catholic experience has a rich tradition. There are many good things about our life and culture that can contribute to rebuilding of religious life in this country. I think it important to pay deliberate, selective (not exclusive!) attention to US resources as we feel and think our way through our refounding.

Sixth, I do believe that "refounding" or "reinventing" comes closer to naming the nature of our challenge than "renewal." Perhaps every era thinks of itself as a watershed time. I believe that globalization and its incredible implications demand refounding. I think, for example, of Karl Rahner's advice to a church that is asked to be a world church in the face of challenges has not seen since the first century. Euro-centric interpretations of God, Christ, churchhood, salvation, etc., should not be imposed upon non-European cultures. The same holds for Euro-centric interpretations of religious life.

Seventh, I will be stressing community and celibacy for the sake of God's reign as exceptionally important defining features of active apostolic communities. And I believe there is some growing consensus around that.

Perhaps, in the German manners of piecing together words to represent a single complex idea, we might add "community-in-permanent-mission" to our lexicon. "Celibate communities in permanent mission" is sort of a root metaphor. Obedience and poverty are characteristics of a community-in-permanent-mission, and take their shape from the nature of the community and how it functions.

Eighth, I am convinced that while the mystical aspect of celibacy and its archetypal religious nature have been abundantly addressed, its pragmatic value to a community-in-permanent-mission may have been slighted. But pragmatically, celibacy can greatly enhance the *disponibilité* of a community-in-permanent-mission. There is no exact English equivalent for this French word. "Available" is the closest, but there is a neutrality about mere availability. When someone is *disponible*, that person is sitting of the edge of the chair, leaning forward into availability. For communities in permanent mission, celibate *disponibilité* has an undeniable strategic value.

Ninth, Greco-Roman culture regarded the human person as "a rational animal." And consequent upon this anthropology, final human fulfillment has been interpreted, for example, as a beatific vision—the contemplation of beauty, truth, and goodness as these are found in God. But an alternative anthropology has been emerging in Western culture, one with significant similarities to the Jewish anthropology from the cultural world of Jesus. This anthropology sees a person as an historical agent who collaborates with her/his brothers and sisters to "make a world." The religious version of this anthropology elevates the human vocation to the level of a collaboration with God in realizing God's intentions for human history. People like Hannah Arendt and the Scottish philosopher John Macmurray have developed this idea, as have religious sociologists like Peter Berger and Joseph Luckmann.

Tenth, I distinguish between a community's "deep story" and charism. The deep story is the narrative structure of a community's life, deeply embedded in its reflected and unreflected instincts. Phenomenologically, that deep story is called charisma or charism only when it responds to people's deeper longings, anguishes, and joys with hope and power. The deep story is validated as charism by those who experience hope and healing when a deep story has gone to work effectively and noticeably. No religious order can, on its own, claim charism. That is a judgment conferred by "others" who have experienced it as great good news.

Eleventh, I will draw upon the experience of small church communities (also known as base communities, small Christian communities, and by other names), and will especially recommend a new kind of centrality to the dialogue between deep story and culture in the everyday religious practices of active apostolic communities.

Twelfth, I will be recommending the daily experience of liturgy of the Word as a principal place where a dialogue between faith and a community's deep story fruitfully, and sometimes fitfully, occurs. The recommendation that this be given a central function in a community's religious practices arises from my experience of small church communities.

Thirteenth, my focus is upon active, apostolic communities and their "worldly" presence. Many of us have borrowed from monastic spiritualities and customs in ways that have not helped us espouse a fully worldly way of life. I believe in the validity of the monastic vocation, its reasons for maintaining monastic enclosure, monastic distance from the world as attendant upon its presence to the world, the power of the Choir in its prayer life, etc. But monastic distance from the world, and the customs and practices that foster it, are not particularly helpful to active apostolic communities.

Fourteenth, and building upon the thirteenth, we are in the world and that's the only place we are. God is in the world, and we need not take leave of the world to encounter God. I believe we can capitalize on what David Tracy identifies as a deep Catholic trait, the analogical imagination, which is our disposition to see God reflected in and through the world. We must be unmistakably world-affirming but not without a highly developed critical sense. However, I hear more of the church's critique of the world than I hear of the world's critique of church. These are two voices that need to be heard interactively.

Fifteenth, I believe that "withness" and "otherness" are coordinate notions. We only know of otherness through the hints we gather from withness. The only trustworthy route to transcendence is through the concreteness of our lived experience, never around it or without it. The "withness" of God in the concreteness of experience is worldly, and is what introduces us to God beyond God, as Paul Tillich names it. "Totally other" may be good poetry about God, but nothing totally other could ever be experienced by us.

Sixteenth, my intellectual formation has been rooted in philosophical theology, and I am sure that shows up throughout the book. I would identify three strains in particular: process theology, hermeneutics, and a wide range of positions often grouped together as postmodern or deconstructionist. I absolutely do not subscribe to the soft relativism that says one position is as good as another. But I do subscribe to the irreducible, non-transcendable historical and cultural shaping of every position. We can never get on top of things without bias. It is painful and deeply religious to assent to finitude or creaturehood and its inherent limitations. Adam ate the apple because he wanted to know in the same way that God knows. The apple is still shiny and fragrant.

Finally, seventeenth. I want to acknowledge the importance of the social sciences to theological reflection and to organizational planning, including refounding. To put it one way, grace is always mediated through socio-historical circumstances (even when I am alone), and anything that elucidates how people function can shed light on the operations of grace.

I was general editor of the seven-volume series, *Alternative Futures for Worship*. Each volume was produced through interaction among three disciplines: the social sciences which described each "slice of life" that forms each sacrament's symbolic mediation, a sacramental theologian who took the social scientific report seriously into her/his sacramental theological reflections, and then a liturgist who imagined ways to ritualize sacramental interpretations that arise from the dialogue between the social scientist and the sacramental theologian.

More recently I was involved as project director of a multi-year study of small Christian communities, generously supported by the Lilly Endowment, Inc. The research was devised and then later interpreted by six theologians, four sociologists, and one anthropologist. This study provided immense insight into what is actually happening, what are the strengths to be supported and the weaknesses to be addressed, and what a better future might look like. The study also funded theological reflection, especially in the area of ecclesiology.

I consider the insights into contemporary religious life from the social sciences absolutely essential to any wise organizational planning. If grace works through nature, we must not do end runs around nature. I am greatly indebted to the extraordinary work, for example, of Patricia Wittberg and Gerald Arbuckle, for their insights into religious life from the perspectives, respectively, of sociology and cultural anthropology.

In chapter two I will make extensive use of the cultural anthropology of Peter Worsley on charisma and of Stephen Crites' philosophical anthropology of sacred and mundane stories (which I have named differently).

These are not topics to be treated seriatim, but as conscious presuppositions at work throughout, some of which will get specific attention later in the text while others will appear as subtext.

Finally, after each chapter there are some items for discussion. While these might provoke personal reflection, they are meant especially for readers who are reflecting on the book together. If they are not the right discussion topics for you and your community, then name your own. In all the questions, "community" can mean your immediate local live-in community, a regional community, the entire religious congregation, etc. Make your own determinations.

FOR DISCUSSION

1. The opening chapter is called "Broken and Building." What are some of your concrete experiences of brokenness, and concrete examples of building?

TWO

Deep Story and the Possibility of Charism

Introduction

"The 'recovery of charism' may be one of the most unsupportable and unnecessary burdens a religious institution has ever been asked to bear, because it cannot be done." I wrote this sentence over a dozen years ago in an article in *Review for Religious* (Lee, 1989, 124-135). I want to take the theme up again with further elaboration.

Charism is not a property. It is not a possession. It is not transferable. It is not transmittable. And it is not controllable. Charism is a radically historicized social phenomenon. It cannot be duplicated in any other time and place. It has never been, in Ernest Hemingway's words about Paris, a moveable feast.

Yet the quest for charism is not misplaced for those who understand that it can only be reinvented, posited, in a new socio-historical setting, but never simply reenacted. Charism is always and only timely and present. It is never a potency awaiting actualization. It is a finite creature born in its own age.

In this chapter I will draw upon resources from both anthropology and sociology to suggest that the popular understanding of charism is more effectively interpreted with two terms instead of one: deep story and charism. By "effectively interpreted" I mean exactly that—an interpretation that can help effect those conditions which may not guarantee charism, but without which it is most unlikely to make an appearance.

Religious orders are part of a sociologically strange and wonderful dimension of Roman Catholic experience, and in their origins they are almost always an effective prophetic presence. Joan Chittister remarks that "religious simply did what was not being done so that others would see the need and do it" (Chittister, 1995, 2). They are important players in a sort of double structure that services the needs of the Reign of God through the church. There is the hierarchical structure with bishops, priests, deacons, parishes, dioceses, archdioceses, bishops' conferences, synods, councils, etc. And there are religious communities of many kinds with convents, cloisters, monasteries, all manner of communities, general chapters, provincial chapters, schools, hospitals, retreat and conference centers, all of which are not hierarchical, though a vital part of the institutional life of the church. Many religious orders have staffed parishes which, though part of the diocesan structure, have been imbued with the spirituality of the religious communities that staff them.

Both of these interrelated structures serve, teach, minister, and evangelize. Sometimes they overlap in strange and helpful ways. For example, in the early history of Christianity in Scotland, the basic structure of the church was related to monasteries and not to dioceses. Even today, some abbots, leaders of monastic communities, have the power to ordain (I was ordained by an abbot in Switzerland).

In an address to the Association of Religious Superiors in Germany, Johannes Metz suggested two major kinds contributions of religious orders to the life of the church: innovative and corrective. The innovative function is to fashion "productive models for the Church as a whole in the business of growing accustomed to living in new social, economic, intellectual and cultural traditions" (Metz, 1978, 11). He acknowledges that the church's record for becoming accustomed to new thinking is not strong. The fear of internal loss of meaning often inclines the institutional church to shut itself off from positive dialogue with new models. The result can be a growing loss of significance. When regular church attendance in the US Catholic Church has dropped from between seventy-five and eighty percent in 1960 (Gallup) to twenty-six-point-seven percent in 1993 (Hadaway), "loss of significance" is probably a fair judgment.

The second thing that initiates, or in some cases reinstitutes, a religious community is a corrective function. "Against the dangerous accommodations and compromises that the Church as a large scale institution can always incline to...[religious communities] press for the uncompromising nature of the gospel and of the imitation of Christ.... They are a kind of shock therapy instituted by the Holy Spirit for the Church as a whole" (Metz, 1978, 12).

The Nygren/Ukeritis study titled *The Future of Religious Orders in the United States* offers a similar interpretation. It claims that "religious orders have classically arisen in the midst of the church to serve emerging or unmet needs" (272). When they do this, they are interacting intimately and effectively with the world around them. I presume that the orders arise because the hierarchical structure does not or cannot respond sufficiently to emerging needs or unmet needs.

While intimately connected to church life, religious orders do not belong to the hierarchical structure, and that is sometimes enough of a marginal edge to enable them to say and do new things. Something very important needs to be done and someone with the requisite know-how chooses to do it. People recognize the importance of what is being done, praise it, are grateful for it, and some join in the doing of it. Charism has happened. When it initiates a community it is a founding charism. When it makes a community re-live again with power, it is a reinvented (not a retrieved) charism.

In this chapter I would like to use what I believe are useful insights from sociology and anthropology to elucidate the nature of charism. Two primary sources will be Stephen Crites' article, "The Narrative Quality of Experience" and Peter Worsley's interpretation of charisma in his book *The Trumpet Shall Sound*.

Theology's Partners: Philosophy and the Social Sciences

Let me say by way of momentary diversion that classical scholastic theology has tended to rely on metaphysics as a special partner, for whatever elucidates the structure of being can help us understand the functional operations of grace, since grace is mediated by historical being. A lot of contemporary theology cannot be understood apart from the social sciences, such as sociology, anthropology, psychology, etc., for these elucidate the human conditions through which and in which grace saves. In this book I am sometimes dialoguing with philosophy and sometimes with the social sciences. In this chapter, the dialogue is with anthropology and sociology.

Two Factors: Charism and Deep Story

The distinction between a community's founding charism and its deep story helps elucidate the nature of charism and also the concrete ways in which charism is reinvented when a community's deep story comes alive in a new way in new time. A deep story is a community's possession in a way that charism "ain't necessarily so." I want to suggest that in every period of an order's historical life, the order incarnates its deep story, but, for reasons that follow in this chapter, not every one of these historical incarnations qualifies as charism.

Throughout this chapter, I will presume the validity of interpreting a religious order as a culture, and will attend to that claim at the end of the chapter. I will begin with Stephen Crites' narrative understanding of culture (Crites, 1971, 291-311).

Style

Crites says that a culture has a style. You can't tell a person's style from a single photograph (how one walks, or talks, or gestures, or one's mannerisms) because "style is in the movement" (292). One has to hang around a person or a culture, or a religious order, and watch it in action to get the hang of it. People in the same culture, with many obvious differences, share a style. While a style might be mimicked, even effectively, it only shapes the heart and mind and body of one who grows up in it, or spends sufficient time in it to get its drift.

In my teaching experience in the university, I have been associated with four religious order: Marianists (my community), Jesuits, Benedictines (men and women), and Religious of the Sacred Heart. Each has stories to tell, especially "creation" stories (how the order was founded, with abundant mythological elaborations), songs to sing, rituals to enact, special words that trigger strong emotions. There are shared memories and shared hopes recognizable to just about all community members.

Music is like that. Vivaldi and Puccini are Italian and no one familiar with music would mistake them for Bach or Bruckner, or for Ravel or Debussy. Yet no composer can write the Italian or German or French symphony that perfectly incarnates the Italian, German, or French style (character), although each gives solid clues, and the more clues the better. Each helps tell the story of its culture, but none exhausts it. One could say the same thing for literature: the *Aeneid*, *Oedipus Rex*, *El Cid*, *Das Nibelungenlied*, *Chanson de Roland*, *Huckleberry Finn*, or *A Streetcar Named Desire*. They all tell some of a culture's story, and hint at that culture's deeper character. No work of literature tells it all, just as no musical composition exhausts a national character.

Deep Story and Particular Story

Crites says that "[sacred] stories seem to be allusive expressions of stories that cannot be fully and directly told, because they live, so to speak, in the arms and legs and bellies of the [tellers]. These stories lie too deep in the consciousness of a people to be directly told: they form consciousness rather than being among the objects of which it is directly aware" (295).

I once took a class in Paul's letters. Members of the class were from different Christian religious traditions. All members of the class used the same text. While there was frequently a consensus about meaning, with equal frequency there was animated, even fierce, debate because vested interests in the nature of the Christian life were at stake in our different interpretations. What we gradually realized was the impact of a Lutheran upbringing, or Presbyterian, or Catholic, or Baptist, upon each one's reading. Lutheran culture brings a different consciousness to the table than Catholic consciousness. While there is, to be sure, some overlap and agreement, there is a different sort of consciousness at work as well. These consciousnesses "and the symbolic worlds they project, are not like monuments that [people] behold, but like dwelling places. People live in them" (Crites, 1971, 295). While I know some things about a Jesuit, Benedictine, or Sacred Heart consciousness, I do not live in them from the inside out. I was not reared in their stories. Acculturated is perhaps the word. I do not feel them the way a "native" feels them. My life has not been created by them.

All of these stories allude to the deep narrative structure of culture, but they do not and cannot tell "the" story that underlies them all. Crites calls a fundamental, formative narrative form that gives a culture its character and its consciousness a "sacred" story, not because it is inherently religious, but because it creates the life we live.

Every story, and every manifestation of a sacred story in a ritual, a custom, a song, etc., Crites calls a "mundane" story since it is the way—the only way—the sacred story makes its appearance in the "world" (*mundus*, world).

To avoid the ease with which the word sacred is equated with religious, and mundane with banal, I will hereafter refer to a sacred story as a deep story, and a mundane story as a particular story.

Every religious order has its deep story. A constitution or a rule of life is a community's attempt to articulate the deep story as effectively as it can. The Church's attempt after Vatican II to tell its deep story in a catechism, like the catechism of Trent that was written after that Council, is an attempt to edge closer to the deep story. But such documents are no sooner produced than we feel their inability to catch the full mystery, even as we respect the attempt. The deep story is more expansive, more elusive, more supple, than any particular story can tell.

The Transformation of a Deep Story

Some start out
with a big story
that shrinks.

Some stories accumulate power
like a sky gathering clouds,
quietly, quietly,
till the story rains around you.

Some get tired of the same story
and quit speaking...
What will we learn today?
There should be an answer
and it should
change.

—Naomi Shihab Nye, *Yellow Glove*

It helps us to know what makes a big story shrink. And what makes a story accumulate power. What makes a story be the kind that doesn't tire? There should be an answer and it should change, because new people are telling it to new people in a new time. It is not really the same story; but, of course, it is.

We know/experience that cultures change at very deep levels. In the McCarthy era in United States history, something as elusive as it was penetrating was transpiring in the psyche of this nation. The fate of Julius and Ethel Rosenberg was part of that anguish. The Camelot aura of the brief Kennedy years signaled a new mood, but mood at quite a deep level of national soul. No one can instigate or control the transformation of a deep or sacred story:

Sacred stories, too, are subject to change, but not by conscious reflection. People do not sit down on a cool afternoon and think up a
sacred story. They awaken to a sacred story, and their most significant mundane stories are told in the effort, never fully successful, to

articulate it. For the sacred story does not transpire within a conscious world. It forms the very consciousness that projects a total world horizon, and therefore informs the intentions by which actions are projected into that world. The style of these actions dance[s] to its music. One may attempt to name a sacred story...but such naming misleads as much as it illuminates, since its meaning is contained—and concealed—in the unutterable cadences and revelations of the story itself. (Crites, 1971, 296)

Reading successive editions of a Rule of Life or Chapter documents in anguished historical times gives clues to changes in the deep story. Deep stories, however, even as they redevelop, elude the best attempts of particular stories to grab them by the throat. Although I do not mean this in a technical psychological sense, I have a feeling that a deep story is sort of midway between a collective unconscious and a collective conscious.

Charisma/Charism

Beginning with Max Weber, there has been an interest among sociologists of religion in the nature of charisma, and there is an extensive literature on the topic. The question, in its early stages, was something like this: What are the observable characteristics of a charismatic person? This is a phenomenological question. Max Weber tended to emphasize the special gifts of mind and body and spirit of a charismatic person. He recognized that a charismatic person's claims break down if they are not recognized by the ones to whom the person feels sent. In a religious context, the charismatic person claims to have received the special gifts and the mission that goes with them from God. I believe that this is the model often invoked by religious communities about their foundress or founder, and often a veritable mythology develops in support of it.

In the material to which I shall refer, the question has shifted, though the approach is still empirical or phenomenological. Instead of asking "what are the characteristics of a charismatic person?" the question shifts to an inquiry into "what is going on in some social context when charisma is attributed to someone?" Here the question is directed to the larger social context in which charisma is experienced, rather than at the person to whom charisma is attributed. This is the approach taken by Peter Worsley in his book, *The Trumpet Shall Sound*.

I will use this framework and apply it not only to the social emergence of a charismatic figure, but also to the social emergence of a charismatic group or community. What is going on in the life of a religious order in some social context that indicates to the popular judgment that charism is at work here?

What I am suggesting is that the founding of religious orders is charismatic in character and that sociologically we are justified in speaking of a founding charism. However, the survival of charism with profound animation and relevance requires subsequent moments that are equally charismatic in character. Subsequent charismatic moments differ dynamically, socially, and historically from the founding charismatic moment. A deep story is not the same as charism. A deep story can survive as an animating narrative with committed followers, and still lack charism. In fact, there can be particular stories that are faithful to the deep story, the narrative structure, but are largely boring and irrelevant. That same particular story may have been exciting and dynamic in another time and or in another place.

Deep stories differ from charism. Unlike charism, deep stories are a kind of possession and property. They are a gift from God. They are truly our inheritance. They have a dynamic and a direction. People can truly, even splendidly, embody the deep story without any conscious awareness that they do it, and without any keenness in articulating it, because their formation "took," and the deep story is embedded in their lives.

A deep story can be transmitted from generation to generation. But charism cannot be transmitted from generation to generation, only reinvented. Charism is fully and radically historicized. It belongs to a time, but one time only. Charism is "constitutively drenched in temporality," to borrow a phrase from Kenan Osborne regarding all human activity (Osborne, 2000, 96). It is also constitutively drenched in locality. We belong to time and to place.

This connection between "charism" and "deep story" sheds some light on the nature of a founding charism and its potential for continuing incarnations. We will look at Worsley's interactionist model of charisma.

An Individualized Interpretation of Personal Charism

Many of our interpretations of our foundresses and founders use the word charism about this key person. Max Weber, one of the early sociologists of religion, formulated a phenomenology of charism that resembles this commonplace interpretation of a charismatic person. Charisma, he wrote, is

> ...a certain quality of an individual personality by virtue of which [such a person] is set apart from ordinary [people] and treated as endowed with supernatural, superhuman, or at least specifically exceptional powers or qualities. These are not accessible to the ordinary person, but are regarded as of divine origin, and on the basis of them he is considered a leader. (Weber, 1947, 358-359)

Further, we frequently attribute timelessness to this charismatic quality and understand it to have been internalized in the life of the community the charismatic person founded.

> ...the charism of a religious community is that gift or combination of gifts which God the Holy Spirit gave to the founding person so that the community might come into existence in the first place....This gift, or special combination of gifts, is not limited by time or culture and is found in, and is enfleshed in, the present day followers of the founding person, enabling them to live his or her vision in our own time. The charism gives the community its basic identity.... (Renfro, 1986, 527-528, emphasis added)

Even as we say such things, we often also say that "he was a man of his time" or that "she was clearly ahead of her time." We also sense the match between and age and its heroes. I think most Americans would say that both John F. Kennedy and Ronald Reagan had charisma. But clearly, these are not interchangeable. Probably neither would have had charism in the other's historical time.

An Interactionist Interpretation of Social Charism

Peter Worsley says that when we identify someone as charismatic, we are really naming that person's effective relationship to a particular social group at a particular historical moment, and likewise the social group's particular kind of relationship to that certain person. It is an interactionist relationship (Worsley, 1968, xiv).

First of all, there is a group of people "with possible utopian or at least diffused and unrealized aspirations" (*ibid.*). There are longings, hungers, needs, perhaps even desperate unmet needs in a social group. And all of those sentiments and passions are there because of social conditions.

Second, there is an individual who is able to articulate a people's aspirations so that when that person names them, the people recognize their story (*ibid.*). Such a person would have to be, in some way, an insider to the experience of the people, one who recognizes the people's longings because he or she has them too, knows them from the inside out, embodies them in his or her own person. The embodiment is powerful, and is the basis for the charismatic leader's ability to function symbolically as the message bearer (Worsley, 1968, xvii).

When this happens in a Judeo-Christian religious context, Abraham Heschel's description of a prophet's religious experience is apropos. While a person may be irate at injustice in his/her own right, what most moves the religious figure is that, based on a profoundly personal relationship with God, that person shares God's feelings, sees the world the way God sees the world, and has a passionate interest in remaking the world because God wants it remade. "[T]he reward and distinction of prophetic existence [is]...to be attuned to God.... The goal of sympathy is not to become like unto God, but to become effective as a prophet through approximation to the pathos of God. In sympathy divine pathos is actually experienced in the moment of crisis..." (Heschel II, 1962, 91, 102-103). The charismatic person sympathizes with both the pain of God and the pain of God's people, and wishes to remedy a situation causing pain and anxiety.

Third, the potentially charismatic leader must be able to convert these aspirations into concrete, visible goals, must "purport to offer the realization of certain values in action" (Worsley, 1968, xii). The nature of a social group's issues is crucial to how leaders are able to mobilize support so readily (Worsley, 1968, xiii).

Fourth, and finally, to become the sort of person that people later call charismatic, the charismatic appeal, "if it is to become the basis of collective social action, needs to be perceived, invested with meaning, and acted upon by significant others.... The charismatic personality has to be 'recognized,' socially validated and accorded the right, firstly, to formulate policy (especially in markedly innovative ways), and then to communicate support for policy" (Worsley, 1968, xi-xii). No one can be charismatic alone. It is not just a matter of personal qualities alone. If there is no following, the word "charisma" will never be invoked to describe a person. To be charismatic, a person's gifts must be socially recognized. "Charisma, therefore, sociologically viewed, is a social relationship, not an attribute of individual personality of a mystical quality" (Worsley, 1968, xii).

Charism is the social reality that provides the setting for a new religious order. It does not exist in the founding person alone, or in the followers, or in the aspirations of the age, or in the style of life proposed, but in the mutual complicity of all of these together.

Every charismatic moment reflects the cry of the age. The cry of one age is never identical to the cry of any other age. To be sure, underlying the cries of all the ages are serious recurrent human concerns; yet in any one time and place, they will never have the same configuration that they had in an other age. That is why a charism is never a moveable feast. It is far too time-bound.

When the foundress or founder begins to make life together with followers, they create among themselves a "style" within which their faith is lived. There is a power, a compelling presence, in what they are up to. It is supported by wide appeal, and may evoke fierce opposition as well. These first members of a community are starting a story. A narrative structure is taking shape. Out of their life together, patterns form. Structures emerge in support of the narrative pattern. Frequently the issues faced by a new community are understood with such ample and accurate generalization that the narrative structure is immensely supple. This narrative structure is the community's deep story, making its first appearance in the founding charism. The deep story can be transmitted. But the moment of charism cannot. Charism can only be reinvented.

I am trying to clarify two distinguishable but related realities. The first is a community's deep story. The deep story is a possession, an inheritance, and is rightly interpreted as God's gift. But whether that story keeps on coming alive through charism depends on whether it can mediate redemption for another age. The deep story emerges again as charism when it is able to rise to the occasion, and when the occasion—which is the contemporary world in all its concreteness— rises in turn to meet it. When these two realities rise up face to face and meet publicly, the world knows it. At that moment redemption has a face and charism happens again and anew. Then one can hear the beating of great wings.

The analysis I have used is about a person judged to be charismatic, and how a number of factors enter into that phenomenon. It is an interactive model, involving the gifts of a person, the needs and hopes of an age, and a powerful and effective connection between them that is publicly perceived and appreciated. When there are people who form community in those historical moments of charism, they start a life and a story together.

All of us in religious life know the life-disconcerting (but life-giving) tension that follows upon the founding of a new community. It is the dialectic between the wildness, as it were, of charism and the need for order. The amazing new Story that is begun cannot be handed on and continued without structures that maintain the story, within which new members can be socialized. The danger is that order and structure will domesticate the deep story and freeze it in a form which was full of power in one age and but does not speak to a new age in the same way. In fact, religious communities can live a long while that way in settled times, but in periods of great transformation and resulting turmoil, communities that cannot make charism happen once more either cease to exist or linger on enfeebled. These patterns are familiar and need not be repeated.

The Future of Religious Orders

I think the Nygren/Ukeritis report, following the Lilly funded study, is exactly right. They suggest that those orders will succeed and survive who can do three things very well. The first of these is responding to critical, unmet human needs, which is another way of naming a very sensitive responsiveness to the cry of the age. Obviously, a community only gets to this place by a profoundly accurate reading of its world based upon it own alert and active insertion in that world, and, indeed, its own identification with the cry of the age. It has learned to articulate its reading of the world and to offer concrete strategies of promise. We should not lose the prophetic élan of this effort.

Walter Brueggemann says that the role of the prophet is to enable people to participate in history in ways that are right (Brueggemann, 1978, 22). The biblical word for a history that is "right" is shalom, which is usually rendered in English as "peace." But shalom means more than simply a lack of discord; the Hebrew word suggests a tensed condition that exists when the conditions that keep a world right (right means according to God's intentions for us) are maintained by constant attention and effort in a very ambiguous world.

In order to have this understanding of the world, members of a religious community will have to be deeply inserted into their own culture, must experience its essential passions. They do not just observe the hungers of the world accurately and objectively in others; they mark them in themselves and feel them as their own. Because they own the experience they are better able to speak a commanding articulation about it, more akin to poetry and strategic planning than to theology or philosophy. They have committed insight into what must be done, and practicable plans of action. When they pray, the "Amen" of others means "you prayed my prayers too." Some folks, then, begin to say "Wherever you go, I will go. Your people shall be my people, and your God my God too," not as an abdication but an assumption of responsibility with others.

The second feature of religious communities that survive and thrive, according to the Nygren/Ukeritis study, is that both the situational reading of the world and the proposed strategies are shaped by the particularity of the deep story in which a community lives and moves and has its being (to borrow Paul's words). The new responding out of an inherited deep story will always involve a reinterpretation of that deep story. This is a deep story's time of openness to creative increment, to the new, to a rewriting, to a new chapter, to additional tradition. A community stays in touch with its historical forms and its historical dreams, wary of nostalgia, which—as Garrison Keillor has reminded us—is another name for poor memory. There never was a perfect golden age, nor shall there ever be. The remembering community studies its documents, researches its spirituality, celebrates its jubilees, asks absolution for its sins, and enjoys its stories. All of that in order to know how to respond, as best it can, to a world it tries to love with God's love.

When I read the multiple articulations of Marianist spirituality, I hear the historical time when each was written. Many of our initial documents are saturated with the spirit of the French revolution. When I read contemporary Marianist documents and know the author, I hear the author's life as well as the community's life (just as my experience biases this book). Albert Schweitzer once remarked that if you want to know someone, get that person to write a life of Jesus. You may not subsequently learn a lot about Jesus, but you'll surely learn a lot about the writer. I believe that in fact one may truly learn a lot about both. If there is no uninterpreted fact (and I know that Nietzsche is correct on this one), then neither is there an uninterpreted tradition.

The third feature of successful reinventions of a religious order is that in all of this a community is informed by its relationship with God. The personal relationship of each member with God is obviously one central feature of a community's relationship with God. I would like to spend some time in this book reflecting upon the nature of a community's social relationship with God. In *Lumen Gentium* we are reminded that it has pleased God to save us, not one by one, but as a people mutually interrelated.

Recall Abraham Heschel's analysis of the prophet as one who has such a personal relationship with God that the prophet knows how God experiences the world, and thus is able to feel the world with

God's feelings. In Hebrew anthropology, this is a coming to know the heart of God. Each religious community shares a tradition about how it prays, and about the nature of common prayer. The challenge in this essay about the religious experience of active, apostolic communities is how a community together comes to feel the feelings of God and then feels the world with God's feelings. This is a different process than that which prompts the individual religious to have that kind of a relationship with God. As a group we covenant with God.

The metaphor for covenant is rooted originally in Near Eastern treaty forms. A king makes a covenant with a people, not with individual members of a nation. The people, once a year, bring out the treaty and read its stipulations to guide them in their relationship with the king and also with each other. The treaty commands a people to have no other king but the covenanting king, and tells the people of mutual obligations among themselves that derive from being a part of the same people related to the same king.

In the highly individualized culture of modern life in the United States, it is not easy to imagine that together we might have the kind of relationship with God that allows us as community to feel the feelings of God, or to identify the structures of common prayer that give us our best chance of doing that.

This is most certainly not an exhaustive list, but some structures of common prayer can be named that nudge deep story into the possible arena of charism:

1. interpreting Scripture communally;
2. interpreting the world we live in communally;
3. interpreting our deep story together;
4. and fashioning from these experiences together the shape of our urgent presence in the world.

If we are sensitive in all of these areas, we might know how to make our deep story mediate the coming-to-be of the Reign of God so that the story becomes charism once again. But it will never be we who can or should call it charism. That is an outside call, if we follow Peter Worsley's understanding of charism.

Recruitment

One of the signs of charism is the presence of a following, especially of those with the particular gifts that fit a deep story. Concern for a following, so that when we are gone others will take up the deep story, is an issue of creativity. Creativity is a healthy sign as long as it is not prized for its own sake.

Like all religious, I want to see my community not only survive, but thrive. But that should not be anyone's first concern. Our first concern is to collaborate with God, as fully as we can, with all we have at our disposal from our deep story and our current resources, to further God's intentions in the world. We, like the church itself, exist for the reign of God and not for ourselves.

Of all orders ever founded, most have ceased to exist. Finitude and creaturehood belong together. This is a painful reality. In his address to religious superiors in Germany, Johannes Metz remarked that sometimes we must have the truth in us to say our time is over. He calls it the *ars moriendi*, the art of dying. Perhaps we need to sanction a ritual akin to anointing (Metz, 1978).

Karl Rahner once spoke about the future as a symbol of God, related to the creative transformation of the world according to God's intentions. The future is not what we plan, although our tools for prediction are to be valued and used; but the future these tools foretell is an extension of the present. The real future, Rahner says, is the one that comes to us in its own time and often leaves our predictions and plans in shreds (Rahner, 1969, 64). What is perhaps most difficult as a way of living in preparation for the real future is letting go of something beautiful which we ourselves have helped create. It must be relinquished, not because it has lost that beauty, but because its time has passed. Some other new beauty is being made.

We can only think thinkables. God does unthinkables. I suppose many of us in religious life suspect that our present situation is one of those unthinkables we did not see coming. We are learning that religious communities will, for the foreseeable future, be both smaller and different. And, having said that, we all know that "recruitment" is vital if we believe that our deep story matters in the world because it serves God's reign. Numbers are a stringent strategic concern. Generativity is a necessary endowment.

If we do all we can to connect our deep story to our perceptions of how God's intentions can be currently served well, then our survival will still be God's gift and not our achievement. It will not be the result of energetic recruitment, though if all else fits, that is a plus.

A Theology of Charism

One of the critiques I sometimes hear of an extensive use of anthropology, or psychology, or sociology, is that it seems to reduce grace to a purely human phenomenon. I want to stress that every experience of God is mediated. When we understand the mediation, we have additional insight into how God's grace is operating right now, how God is addressing us right now. In an epilogue to *I and Thou*, Martin Buber says that people often ask him why God seemed to have spoken so much and so clearly a thousand, and two thousand and three thousand years ago, but is not heard today. Buber says the reason is that we think God will speak either above or alongside everyday life, when in fact everyday life, when it calls us to decision, is the personal speech of God (Buber, 1958, 136-137).

In one of his very early works, *Hearers of the Word*, Karl Rahner observes that "revelation is essentially a historical process. That and how it took place depends strictly on a unique combination of historical events, in which God's work has authentically spoken to humanity.... Therefore turning toward history is not something optional for us" (Rahner, 1994, 7, 136). For us as Christians, the New Testament is our most important resource for understanding God's intentions for the world. The personal speech of God is especially "loud" when some present social situation is either deeply faithful to God's intentions, and asks our support, or is deeply contrary to God's intentions, and asks for intervention. God speaks to individuals and to communities in these ways. "Thus the place of a possible revelation is always and necessarily also our history" (Rahner, 1994, 94).

The same historical events will frequently be listened to theologically in a great variety of ways. There is no uninterpreted experience.

All our past histories, our psychological makeup, our loves and our hates, the time and place in which we live, language itself, shape our listening. How Sisters of St. Joseph, Franciscans, Jesuits, Mercy Sisters, Marianists, Christian Brothers, et al., listen is always shaped by their deep stories, just as their responses will then be shaped by the same deep story, because the Spirit works through who we are, never around who we are, yet it is still the work of the Spirit. "The charism of religious life," writes Pope John Paul II, "far from being an impulse born of 'flesh and blood,' or one derived from a mentality which conforms to the modern world, is the fruit of the Holy Spirit, who is always at work within the church" (*Evangelica Testificatio*, 11).

The Immediately Following Chapters

The next two chapters are meant to be a serious response to the following directives in *Perfectae caritatis*:

> Therefore, drawing on the authentic sources of Christian spirituality, let the members of communities energetically cultivate the spirit of prayer and the practice of it. In the first place they should take the Sacred Scriptures in hand each day by way of attaining "the excelling knowledge of Jesus Christ" (Phil. 3:8) through the reading of these divine writings and meditating on them. They should enact the sacred liturgy, especially the most holy mystery of the Eucharist, with hearts and voices attuned to the Church; here is a most copious source of nourishment for the spiritual life. (*Perfectae caritatis*, 6)

Whatever else communities may do, respective of their deep stories and particular customs, liturgy of the Word and Eucharist are to be central. How that centrality functions is up to each religious order, always with appropriate adapations to the local level.

The next chapter will address the liturgy of the word, taking into account recent biblical scholarship. The chapter which follows that will address the Eucharist.

FOR DISCUSSION

1. Name some of the key elements that you believe are essential pieces of your deep story. If you do this as a group, what are the areas of strong agreement? Are there any disputed points?

2. What are some "critical, unmet human needs" to which your deep story has something redemptive to say?

3. Do you sense some directive for mission when you put the answers to #1 and #2 together? Or even strategies?

4. What are some stories (from the congregation's history or from your lifetime) that you feel resonate especially strongly with your deep story?

THREE

THE WORD'S ADDRESS
TO COMMUNITY

The word of God is the first source of all Christian spirituality. ...Meditation on the Bible in common is of great value. *Vita consecrata*, #94

Formation is a dynamic process by means of which individuals are converted to the word of God in the depths of their being and at the same time learn how to discover the signs of God in earthly realities. *Vita consecrata*, #68

...the supreme rule of the religious life and its ultimate norm is that of following Christ according to the teaching of the Gospel. *Evangelica testificatio*, #12

[Religious life is] a permanent element in the history of the Church: the host of founders and foundresses, of holy men and women who chose Christ by radically following the Gospel and by serving their brothers and sisters, especially the poor and the outcast. *Vita consecrata*, #5.

Introduction

This chapter is an unabashed pitch for giving to Scripture a place of privilege it has never had in the regular prayer life and spirituality of active apostolic communities. This is a response partly to the recovery of a central emphasis on Scripture in the Second Vatican Council, partly to the emphasis upon Word in post-conciliar documents on religious life, and partly to major advances in biblical scholarship in the twentieth century—advances that "access" the Christ event in ways full of delight and surprise and incredible power.

In fact, the achievements of biblical scholarship are part of the reason for the Church's new emphasis on Scripture. The point is not simply the value of scholarship, but that this scholarship helps our ears better hear biblical texts speak today with their original voice and power. In a 1993 document, *Interpretation of the Bible in the Catholic Church*, the Pontifical Biblical Commission warns against an easy literal reading of biblical texts, saying that it is tantamount to intellectual suicide.

The texts given at the beginning of this chapter also say that biblical prayer goes hand in hand with discovering what God is saying through earthly realities.

The Scriptures arose out of community. They came into being for the sake of community. Reading and pondering the Scriptures in community honors their communal origins and communal intentions. Some of the most significant progress in this regard has occurred in the life of small Christian communities, and I have them in mind often in this book.

Presence

I want to begin with some conversation about the meaning of the word "presence." First of all, I take presence to be dialogic. I do not mean the mere "thereness" of something. If something is "there" and I do not know it, and it does not impinge on me in any way, there is no experience of presence. Nor do I mean spatial nearness. A friend who is miles away can be "nearer" to heart and mind than the person sitting next to me in the theatre or at church. Nor do I mean temporal nearness. When I account for who I am today, my parents, neither of whom is living, are far more present in my life than any number of people whom I have recently met. Presence corresponds to whatever has a hold on my becoming. Likewise, presence is whatever has a hold on a community's becoming.

Our focus in this chapter will be upon the power of the Word to shape religious communities. In the following chapter we will look at presence in the context of Eucharist. Another clear concern is how the handling our community's deep story will make it effectively present to our current dialogue with the world. The availability of key documents is essential, for example, but they come alive most when they are conversation partners with Word and/or mission.

The interesting contrast is not between presence and absence, but between low-density presence and high-density. Someone may have been baptized Catholic, but if Catholic faith does not exercise a hold on the person's becoming, it is either of minimal density, or perhaps no longer exists.

God is. The Christ event has actually occurred. The Spirit is everywhere. Absence is not an issue. They are there all the time. But presence happens when God exercises a hold on our becoming, when God makes a difference, when the Christ-event clarifies God's intentions in specific events, when the Spirit creates in us an appetite for God. What really matters is how strong a hold this presence exerts on our becoming. God's self-gift is always ready-to-hand. It awaits our welcoming it into our becoming.

We will first have a brief conversation with Paul concerning the Word-presence of God:

> How then are they to call on him if they have not come to believe in him? And how will they hear of him unless there is a preacher for them? And how will there be preachers if they are not sent? (Rom 10:14)

The point is clear: faith arises in response to the Good News about Jesus Christ. But one doesn't lead a Christian life through having heard the Word just once. It is the constant effective contact of the Word with our living that increases the density of God's presence to us. Effective is the key word here—having effects, having a hold on our becoming. The way in which small Christian communities celebrate the Word is certainly instructive for all Christians, but has particular relevance for communities of religious. Let us imagine such a gathering.

A Model for Word

A genuine Word presence means that Word has a hold on the becoming of someone. It calls Christian life into existence in the first place, and needs to continue happening to keep making Christian life continue being Christian life.

The small Christian community Word dynamic is a model for the prayer experience in religious communities. About a dozen adults have gathered on a Friday evening. After a short time for social amenities, the community leader or the presider for the evening calls the community to gather. Often they take a few minutes at the beginning to catch up on personal news or name significant world news of which Christians should be aware. Sometimes then there is some singing to set the mood and quiet the minds and hearts. After an opening prayer the lectionary readings for Sunday will be proclaimed. The text we shall examine is from Matthew:

> Jesus began to speak to them in parables once again. "The kingdom of heaven may be compared to a king who gave a feast for his son's wedding. He sent his servants to call those who had been invited, but they would not come. Next, he sent some more servants with the words: "Tell those who have been invited: look, my banquet is all prepared, my oxen and my fatted calf have been slaughtered, everything is ready. Come to the wedding." But they were not interested. One went off to his farm, another to his business, and the rest seized his servants, maltreated them, and killed them. The king was furious. He dispatched his troops, destroyed those murderers and burnt the town. Then he said to his servants: "The wedding is ready; but as those who were invited proved unworthy, go to the main crossroads and invite everyone you can find to come to the wedding." So these servants went out onto the roads and collected everyone they could find, bad and good alike; and the wedding hall was filled with guests. (Mt 22:1–10)

There is a short period of quiet to ponder the passage. Then one person says she remembers from the third grade an unpopular girl whose mother had a birthday party for her. The class was invited and only two people showed up. She recalled how sad and shaken the little girl was, and how angry her mother was. She said the king must have felt terrible for his son and his bride. Another person says he's glad that the kingdom of God is like a banquet. He likes parties and people, so that is a good omen. Another agrees, saying that the banquet metaphor for the kingdom is very inviting. Still another names the violence in the story, and feels put off by it: servants are killed, and the king destroys them and burns their town. Another person says that those invited were the Jews, and since they didn't respond to Jesus, he invited everyone else.

Apart from insight into the parable (or lack of it), one important thing going on here is that each time that people speak, they are almost certainly disclosing themselves as well as commenting upon the text. People's own stories get told when, aloud, they probe Scripture together. That in itself is a community-building dynamic.

The facilitator then asks, "Based on what we've said here so far, what's the point of the story, and how might we respond?" The conclusion is that "the reign of God is meant to be a happy experience (banquet), and to include a lot of people." Someone suggests the importance of being responsive to invitations from others to form relationships and of enjoying each other's company.

The community has several commentaries on Matthew's gospel, and on the New Testament more generally. The facilitator is always responsible for doing some "homework" ahead of time on the text. It is often not easy to hear a text from another culture, a different language, and a far distant time the way the original writers would have intended it, or the way the original hearers would have heard it. And if they would have heard it differently than we hear it now, would their conclusions about what the texts mean differ from ours?

The small community facilitator for this Friday evening has done her homework. She is concerned first of all to say that the interpretation about Jews refusing the invitation so others get it instead is not surprising since that kind of interpretation has haunted Christian history and is partly responsible for anti-Semitism. Jesus never stopped being a Jew all his life in all he said and did and was. The one who made the original comment is both a little embarrassed and very much relieved (and will probably never say that again!). Besides that, the two groups often in conflict in Matthew are not Christians and Jews, but Jews who accept the messiahship of Jesus and Jews who do not. But at this early time, both groups are entirely within the Jewish community.

The facilitator who read John Dominic Crossan's commentary on this passage rephrases it in her own words (Crossan, 1994, 66-74). "Sociologists," she says, "call the pattern of people who regularly gather together for meals 'commensality,' i.e., the pattern of gathering in a society." Sociologists also say that regular table fellowship is a reflection of a society. Who gathers with whom at table? Who is never there at table? These are social patterns that structure the world we live in.

In first-century Mediterranean culture, the rules of table fellowship were very strict. But this king says to invite everybody, the good and the bad. This is a radical restructuring of commensality and therefore a radical transformation of cultural patterns, and would have been stunning to its hearers. It would have shaken them up. If you have company for a meal and someone knocks at the door, asking for a handout for food, would you invite that person to share your table with you and your guests?

This small Christian community pondering this passage suddenly recognizes how homogeneous its membership is. Someone suggests that they should examine their recruitment practices. It is perhaps time, he says, deliberately to invite folks who are very different. They resolve to do this, and set their next gathering time aside to work out strategies for doing this. Each community member commits to coming to the next meeting with at least two suggestions for how to approach the issues. These are concrete resolutions.

But there is also some realism. One member, a social worker, asks the community whether, as a group, they are ready to face the ambiguities that will certainly emerge from a more heterogeneous group. She wants to make sure that they understand their own background and biases as they consider making radical changes.

Look at the pattern. People listen and then give their initial responses to what they heard. And they ask how that hearing might shape their responsiveness. They are getting grounded in their present experience, after hearing through their contemporary ears. Then they are told that there are some cultural meanings at work behind the text, e.g., how structured and strict table fellowship was in first-century Mediterranean culture. Then they see meaning in the text in a new way, in their case how communities can be formed in counter-cultural ways, which prepare us ready for the kingdom of God. And that develops different meanings for them in front of the text than they had originally pondered.

Now, to be sure, sometimes the text's meaning is truly obvious and simply stated, and we have reasonably authentic access to it. But often the commentaries, which make available important biblical scholarship, open up meanings and possibilities we never imagined.

A *Dabhar* Kind of Word

"Word of God" is a very common expression in both the Old Testament and the New. The Hebrew word for "word" is *Dabhar*, but it has meanings that are very different from the English "word." When one speaks a *dabhar*/word it is like the self of the speaker going out there into the world and leaving a mark with what is said. It causes something to exist. In fact, *dabhar* can even mean a "thing," that which is brought into existence by the speaking.

In German, *dabhar* is sometimes translated as *Tatwort*, which combines two ideas into one word: "deedword." The *dabhar*/word has effects. When Isaac was tricked by Joseph to give him the blessing that belonged to Esau, Esau then asked his father, "have you not reserved a blessing for me?" In sadness and tears, Isaac remained silent. When he spoke the words the blessing happened, and a fact cannot be made into an nonfact. That's not our way of thinking, but it is a biblical way of thinking.

In that biblical sense, when we proclaim the Scriptures and then say, "The Word of the Lord," we are engaging a narrative that tells of a time past when God's Word had effects. And therefore it is not incorrect to call the text "The Word of the Lord." But it becomes *Word* in the fullest sense when it confronts our contemporary lived experience and moves us to act upon it in ways consistent with its original effects. The image sometimes used in Latin American small communities is that people gather after the sun goes down to address all that happened when the sun was high, and they do not retire until tomorrow's agenda takes shape.

This kind of dialectic requires not only a solid interpretation of Scripture, but an insightful and accurate understanding of our contemporary experience. In his book on biblical community, Paul Hanson writes:

> Utmost care must be given to both sides of the two dimensional exegesis. As much harm can be done by applying an inadequately understood Word to a well-understood world as in applying a well-understood word to an inadequately understood world. (Hanson, 1987, 529)

In the Word/prayer of religious communities, there is a triple exegesis. We facilitate an ongoing dialogue between Scripture, the world, and our community's deep story, and we work for an outcome that is faithful to all three.

The function of a homily is to connect the Scripture with present experience in ways that give concrete direction to our living. It is frankly very rare to hear a homily that does this effectively, often because the biblical homework was not done, but sometimes simply for the reason that the best homilist in the world cannot make connections to the experiences of many people in the liturgical assembly. And in the best of circumstances, when a sensitive homilist has a solid understanding of the assembled community, it is still a traditional educational model: one person tells the others what something means. As we know from educational theory, when people participate actively in their learning experience, they learn more quickly. The small community experience is that sort of intentional Word-community. The processing that a community does to access meaning creates something like an intentional homiletic community. Religious communities have life forms that open us to being homiletic communities.

While the scriptural Word has a pre-eminence, I am also using it as a metaphor. God speaks in many ways. All the resources of our faith and its traditions are words that dialogue with experience: liturgy, spirituality, doctrine, theology, and so on. These are all important words for us.

My fervent hope is that every religious community would pray the Word this way regularly, always invoking the three-fold exegesis of biblical text, world, and deep story. A yearly chapter could be the occasion when they would all come together and tell each other what they have learned about the relevance of their deep story to the Word and the world. Mission wells up therefrom. I would bet that the beating of great wings would be heard.

An Exegetical Approach

Even in conversation with friends, understanding an "other" is not easy. I must let the other's words mean what they mean to him/her, not what I want them to mean. Often the reason that words can have different meanings is that they are associated with different experiences.

In making sense of the small community research with which I have been recently involved, Hispanic theologians on the team reminded others of us that in Anglo culture people instinctively think of individual persons as the basic units of society, while Hispanics tend to think of the family as the basic unit. In that case, the word "family" has very different sociological and emotional weight in one culture than in the other. One of my parents is Hispanic, and when I heard this distinction made I easily saw the differences between my Hispanic family on the one side and my Anglo family on the other side. But I would never have seen this so clearly without help in reading, as it were, "behind the text."

The example above is a simplification of a model that addresses three areas: what is going on behind the text? what is the meaning within the text? and what are the implications in front of the text? To understand a gospel report on Jesus, we need to ask, what's going on behind the text? Why do Mark, Matthew, and Luke each relate a little differently the same basic story? What exactly is the function of the Pharisees and Sadducees in the Judaism of Jesus' time? Why is no account of the resurrection identical with any of the other three accounts? What information can be garnered from extra-biblical materials? What was the role of women in first-century Palestinian Jewish life? Cultural anthropologists insist on the importance of the fierce honor code of first-century Mediterranean cultures, and how it shaped people's expectations and reactions. This kind of explication helps a text speak more clearly with its original voice.

Very few contemporary American women, for example, would understand what it meant for a Jewish woman of the first century to be healed of chronic hemorrhaging. A woman with a flow of blood could not touch or be touched by anyone. No one could sit with her at table, or on the same piece of furniture with her. She was virtually a social outcast for twelve years because of laws set forth in Leviticus, prohibiting a woman with a flow of blood any social contact whatsoever. The healing, then, was not just physical but also social. A social outcast is now able to be reintegrated into normal social relations. Most Americans hearing this story would rejoice that the woman was healed, but few would ever know about her reintegration into normal social relations. For twelve years the people who loved her could not touch her, or eat with her, or sit close to her.

Understanding the social and religious context enriches the meaning of the story, but it also changes our agenda in front of the text, namely, not only to be a healing presence, but to finding ways to integrate those who are most excluded from normal society (physically disabled, homosexuals, very elderly, certain ethnic identities).

The same exegesis is needed when a religious congregation probes its own deep story. My experience of my own community's "story" calls to mind the observation of Patricia Wittberg that "accounts of a religious congregation's foundation, especially when written by the congregation's own members, have often gone to the opposite extreme and have tended to overemphasize the individual and the supernatural at the expense of the social" (Wittberg, 1996, 8).

I belong to one of the multiple new religious orders founded in France in the aftermath of the French Revolution. We do not have an analysis of our origins written by someone technically trained in historiography. Many existing accounts stress Blessed William Joseph Chaminade's reaction to the excesses of the French Revolution, and to the "philosophers" of the enlightenment. But what is missing is an appreciation of the events of that period from the perspective of those who participated in these events. It was the end of the feudal system as a social model and the beginning of a search for participative models. A sensitive person cannot live in an era like this and remain untouched by the deeper strains of what is happening.

As a religious order, the Society of Mary made substantial moves to incorporate many of the ideals of *liberté, fraternité, egalité* (an order in which the ordained have no privileged status in respect to the non-ordained). But the supernatural stories have overshadowed historical analysis of, events. Our communities' deep stories deserve the same kind of exegetical attention that biblical narratives have been receiving. As members of these communities, we need to apply exegetical questions to the stories of our own beginnings.

Meaning in Front of the Text (Pastoral Action)

We are all familiar with the distinction between theory and the application of theory to practice. There is an understanding in Aristotle which calls this model into question, and one that I believe has some surprising affinity for the American spirit.

In the first place, however, Aristotle has a concept of *theoria*, grounded in a Greek anthropology, that I do not accept. The mind, he holds, is made for the contemplation of truth, beauty, and goodness. A theoretical understanding of first causes and natures is a contemplative act that fulfills human existence. For Aristotle, this is the highest kind of knowledge. It has no relationship to the practical world and its daily tasks. To this my American soul does not subscribe.

The second kind of knowledge he calls *phronesis*, and the practical side of that knowledge is *praxis*. *Phronesis* is knowledge of the kind of world we should be making together, a knowledge shaped by our concrete experience of the world, and also by whatever knowledge we brought with us that world. The rhythm of action/reflection is relentless. *Praxis* is our practical action to bring the right kind of world into existence.

All of this discussion occurs in the context of a work on ethics which addresses the question of what constitutes a virtuous person. No one can be a virtuous person without a right understanding of the kind of world we should be making.

Christians believe that God has intentions for the world, and that he requires our collaboration for those intentions to be realized. For us, it is the dialogue between the word and the world that clarifies both God's intentions and how they should be implemented. One cannot at the same time know God's intentions and understand how they can be implemented and not be engaged

In *Lumen gentium* the Second Vatican Council offers an important insight into God's intentions:

> It has pleased God, however, to make us holy and save us not mere-
> ly as individuals without any mutual bonds, but by making us into
> a single people, a people which acknowledges him in truth and
> serves him in holiness. (#9)

Gerhard Lohfink makes a similar point in his study of *Jesus and Community* (Lohfink, 1984). While Jesus' compassion was certainly operative in all the healings, we do not find him taking credit. Often he says, "Your faith has healed you." And sometimes people in the crowd say, "The kingdom of God is here."

In a sort of inaugural address in Luke's gospel, Jesus says that the Spirit is upon him, and in the words of Isaiah 61, "he has sent me to bring good news to the oppressed...to proclaim liberty to captives, and release to the prisoners; to proclaim the year of the Lord's favor." Jesus proclaims and initiates what God is doing for the people with whom he is covenanted. And when individuals are healed, it is because they belong to the people to whom the year of the Lord is happening. Covenant is the root metaphor for God's relationship with us. In this metaphor, a king makes a treaty with a people as a people, not with individuals.

While God indeed has relations with us one by one, he saves us as a people. "City" is a helpful metaphor for how a people shares a destiny. People live together in a city and are connected in their efforts to make the city serve their communal interests. That requires collaboration, which in turn requires sustained conversation, compromises, agreements, and implementation, so that the social system serves the good of the people. The Greek word for city is *polis*, and everything that pertains to the city is political. Because politics is the only way we can serve the needs of social systems, both Aristotle (in *Nicomachean Ethics*) and Thomas Aquinas (in his treatment of "Prudence" in the *Summa Theologica*) say that politics is a virtue (a far cry from many contemporary views of politics).

That was a long *discursus*, perhaps, to say that the inherently political character of a faith that attends to God's intentions for the world is well served by a dialogue between word and world that occurs in a community. And for us who want to put the resources of our deep story at the disposal of God's intentions, there is another reason for reading the Bible and the world and our deep story together.

I know from my experience in communities of religious life and in small Christian communities that finding consensus in our reading of word and world and deep story is neither easy nor painless. We become aware quickly that just as there is no uninterpreted fact, there is also no uninterpreted access to word or world or deep story. It is only through tolerance of ambiguity that we learn to work together for the common good of God's people, and do so, as best we can, on God's terms. A community without a strong prayer life will probably not survive.

Hermeneutics and Pastoral Action

In a section of Martin Heidegger's magnum opus, *Being and Time*, there is a paragraph about "projection" that has implications for the philosophy of interpretation (Heidegger, 1996, pp. 134-144, sections. 31-32). To understand the metaphor of projection, think of the way that a projector projects images upon a screen out in front of it. It is a simple and powerful notion.

Every thing we come to know has some effect on how we see the

world. The effects may be large or small, may be challenging or rein-
forcing. How we see the world always influences how we put life
together in the world. That is the projection part of interpretation, the
real or possible effects out in front of us. That projection belongs to
the meaning structure of whatever it is that we are interpreting. That
sort of understanding is behind the conviction that only when the
word has entered our lived experience is its full meaning as Word
apparent. God's Word intends a world into being. "God said, 'Let
there be light.' And there was light."

Even before Martin Heidegger and the hermeneutical theory of his
disciple Hans-Georg Gadamer, a similar instinct was at work in American
thought. In a well-known essay, "How to make our ideas clear," Charles
Sanders Pierce says that if you want to know what an idea means, see
what it does, what habits of action it produces (Pierce, 1958, 123).

William James further develops the thought in *Pragmatism*. He says
that to learn what something means, we must put it to work in the
stream of experience, and if any two ideas have the same effects, they
mean about the same thing (James, 1975, 26, 25). There are, of course,
some very crass, merely instrumentalist ways of taking this. But they
reflect a truth, that ideas have consequences, and the consequences do
elucidate their meaning, though perhaps not exhaustively. One safe-
guard is to be clear about both short-term consequences and long-term
consequences. Part of the logic of the US using the atomic bomb is that
it saved lives by ending the war sooner, and that is probably true. But
suppose we had chosen not to use the bomb because we felt that we
wanted to live in a world where no one used weapons like this; in that
case we would occupy a higher moral ground today on the issue.

I bring this up because a passion for understanding and dealing
with the consequences of the Word is a gift that American religious
can help bring to the liturgy of the word: an impatience with discussion and sharing that does no actualizing vis-à-vis God's intentions
for our world.

Formation for the Conversation between Word and World

The implementation of such development requires formation and education as well as experiment and experience. In many ways, the small Christian community experience in Latin America and Africa is considerably ahead of that in the United States. Latin America, especially, is more seasoned by time. The conversation between the Word and the world, which implicates us in pastoral strategies, is developed in the political theology of Europe (e.g., Johannes Metz and Hans van der Ven), the theology of liberation in Latin America (e.g., Leonardo Boff and Gustavo Gutierrez), pastoral theology in Africa (Joseph Healy, Gerald West), and in the growing development of practical theology in the United States (e.g., Don Browning, David Tracy, Terry Veling, Rebecca Chopp, and some of my own work). Each of these approaches is a version of making the kind of meaningful correlations between the Bible and concrete experience that elucidates and promotes concrete Christian living. Gutierrez says that the value of this theological method is precisely because it has the same basic structure as Christian life.

I agree strongly with the recommendation of Sandra Schneiders that all religious today should have a Masters of Arts degree in some area of pastoral theology. We expect that of lay women and men who are ministry professionals in contemporary Catholicism, and not just for those in educational apostolates. Indeed, it is not my suggestion that everyone becomes a scholar in biblical exegesis. The normal Scripture courses in many masters' programs give people the background to help lead a community in its conversation between Word and world. This would provide enough trained readers to help all of us ordinary readers approach Scripture in the ways described above.

To help small Christian communities in Brazil, a program of formation is in place, the Centro de Estudos Biblicos, to help the poor and oppressed approach Scripture from a perspective that lets the Bible speak to the particularities of their situation. A program with similar concerns was founded in South Africa, the Institute for the Study of the Bible. Gerald West says that "the primary aim of the ISB is to establish an interface between biblical studies and ordinary readers of the Bible in the church and community that will facilitate social transformation" (West, 1995, 219). He enumerates four commitments that underpin this effort, and I substitute our context for that of Africa:

1. A commitment to read the Bible in community with others.
2. A commitment to read the Bible critically, i.e., attentive to historical biblical criticism.
3. A commitment to both personal and social transformation clarified through contextual Bible study.
4. A commitment to read the Bible from the perspective of the US American context, particularly from the perspective of those who are poor and oppressed (in this country and elsewhere) and to understand the middle and upper class in relation to the whole in this country.

There are many among us in religious life able to lead and conduct such an effort. This conversation also requires skills in social analysis. But once again there are those among us, especially those engaged in social work, who have these skills. They do not have to be the highly sophisticated skills of a sociologist, though those are certainly helpful. I have watched organizations like the Industrial Areas Foundation lead uneducated people to engage in astute social analysis.

The Catholic Church in the United States is probably the best educated national Catholic constituency that has ever existed. There are about three thousand men in graduate seminary programs preparing for ordination, and over six thousand women and men, not on an ordination track, in graduate theology programs.

There is so much need and so much possibility open to us, and religious can certainly be prophetic in this regard. Sadly, it remains rare to hear a homily that is both biblically informed and in explicit touch with the particularities of the assembly gathered. I do not underestimate the time and education it would take to make many of these moves possible, nor do I underestimate the resistance to such major retooling. Many of our past interactional habits are embedded in patterns from a different time and a different church, and from different understandings of Scripture.

Reading the Bible Together: The Community and Truth

The Greek word for truth, *aletheia*, has an interesting etymology. In Greek mythology, the river Lethe separates the earth from the underworld, Hades. Occasionally someone, like Orpheus, was allowed to return from Hades back to life on earth. But it was important that no one from Hades would disclose its secrets. When one crossed the river Lethe, there was an immediate forgetfulness of Hades. Everything about Hades was hidden from consciousness in the crossing of Lethe. The word *Lethe*, therefore, means hiddenness or concealment.

Often in English we put non- before a word to negate it, as in non-flammable. The negating prefix in Greek is the letter alpha. So the Greek word for truth, *aletheia*, means bringing something out of concealment, luring it out of its hiddenness. There is such a fullness of meaning in Scripture that it can never be fully explicated. Scripture can never be turned inside out so that nothing remains hidden. One never "gets it" once and for all. It never, never tells all its secrets.

But when a community interprets Scripture together, it stands a solid chance of bringing its social meanings out of hiddenness through a social act: interpreting together. There is a different kind of disclosure in a community dynamic than in personal reflection. Both are utterly essential. But when a community has a sense that God speaks to its institutional life, to its deep story, it needs ongoing communal interpretation to probe and promote its shared inner life and shared mission.

In the list of resources below, a very select list, I have stressed commentaries that address the social staging wherein the text is found, the social setting that frames its original voice. Some of these resources also probe the contemporary social implications of Scripture, based upon resonances between social phenomena then and now. While these are certainly relevant to any individual's exploration of Scripture, they may be especially helpful where a communal reading of Scripture is concerned.

It is not an easy journey from personal reading or homilies by individuals to learn and love the processes of communal interpretation of our sacred texts, for we are without reliable historical models. Nevertheless, the payoff is worth the effort, if great wings are to be stirred into beating.

FOR DISCUSSION

1. The Catholic recovery of Scripture has been one of the graces of the Church after Vatican II. How has that shown up in the prayer life of your community, and in your own prayer life?

2. How has the world of contemporary biblical studies affected your sense of how God's Word spoke then, and speaks now?

3. Make some concrete suggestions for how to effectively promote an informed conversation between Word and world (the Bible in one hand and the newspaper in the other) in your community.

4. Whether the text is Scripture, church documents, or documents from your religious order, perhaps the most difficult part of interpretation is the "meaning in front of the text," i.e., how its meaning impinges upon the future. Choose some text from your community's recent life and probe its meaning "out in front" of you as a community and individually.

RESOURCES

There are some remarkable resources available for those of us who want to entertain a new kind of sustained, interactive relationship with the Bible so that it might nurture us in soul and in mission. I will indicate first those resources prepared especially for use in small Christian communities, which focus upon the lectionary readings for Sundays.

I will then indicate a number of commentaries that are helpful in situating texts socially and culturally in their original setting, and in applying them to contemporary situations. This bibliography is specifically for the Christian Scriptures. It is obviously quite select and, to be sure, reflects the preferences of the bibliographer. When I teach New Testament to graduate students in pastoral ministry, these are the kinds of material I recommend for introducing people to a more informed dialogue with the sacred texts.

NEW TESTAMENT BIBLIOGRAPHY

Lectionary Guides Specifically for Use in Small Groups

At Home with the Word, Liturgy Training Publications, 1800 North Hermitage Avenue, Chicago, IL 60622-1101.

Exploring the Sunday Readings (monthly), Twenty-Third Publications, PO Box 180, Mystic, CT 06355.

Prayer Time: Faith Sharing Reflections on the Sunday Gospels, RENEW International, Plainfield, NJ, www.renewintl.org

Pilch, John J., *The Cultural World of Jesus: Sunday by Sunday*, Collegeville, MN: The Liturgical Press, 1995.

Quest: A Reflection Booklet for Small Communities, Pastoral Department of Small Christian Communities, Archdiocese of Hartford, 467 Bloomfield Ave., Bloomfield, CT 06002.

Spirit (for youth), Sisters of St. Joseph, 1884 Randolph Ave., St. Paul, MN 55105.

Sunday by Sunday (for adult groups), Sisters of St. Joseph, 1884 Randolph Ave., St. Paul, MN 55105.

Social Context and Social Implications

The Gospel of Matthew

Carter, Warren. *Matthew and the Margins: A Sociopolitical and Religious Reading*. Maryknoll, NY: Orbis Books, 2000.

Crosby, Michael H. *House of Disciples: Church, Economics, and Justice in Matthew*. Maryknoll, NY: Orbis Books, 1988.

Overman, J. Andrew. *Church and Community in Crisis: The Gospel According to Matthew*. Harrisburg, PA:Trinity Press International, 1996.

_____. *Matthew's Gospel and Formative Judaism: The Social World of the Matthean Community*. Minneapolis: Fortress Press, 1990.

Saldarini, Anthony J. *Matthew's Christian-Jewish Community*. Chicago: Univ. of Chicago Press, 1994.

The Gospel of Mark

Blount, Brian K. *Go Preach! Mark's Kingdom Message and the Black Church Today*. Maryknoll, NY: Orbis Books, 1998.

Horsley, Richard A. *Hearing the Whole Story: the Politics of Plot in Mark's Gospel*. Louisville, KY: Westminster John Knox Press, 2001.

Myers, Ched. *Binding the Strong Man: a Political Reading of Mark's Story of Jesus*. Maryknoll, NY: Orbis Books, 1988.

Myers, Ched, et al. *Say to This Mountain: Mark's Story of Discipleship*. Ed. by Karen Lattea. Maryknoll, NY: Orbis Books, 1996.

Sabin, Marie Noonan. *Reopening the Word: Reading Mark as Theology in the Context of Early Judaism*. New York: Oxford University Press, 2002.

Waetjen, Herman C. *A Reordering of Power: A Socio-Political Reading of Mark's Gospel*. Minneapolis, MN: Fortress Press, 1989.

The Gospel of Luke

Cassidy, Richard J. *Jesus, Politics and Society: a Study of Luke's Gospel*. Maryknoll, NY: Orbis Books, 1978.

Esler, Philip Francis. *Community and Gospel in Luke-Acts: The Social and Political Motivations of Lucan Theology*. New York: Cambridge University Press, 1987.

Reid, Barbara E. *Choosing the Better Part? Women in the Gospel of Luke*. Collegeville, MN: Liturgical Press, 1996.

The Gospel of John

Brown, Raymond E. *The Community of the Beloved Disciple*. New York: Paulist Press, 1979.

Cassidy, Richard J. *John's Gospel in New Perspective: Christology and the Realities of Roman Power*. Maryknoll, NY: Orbis Books, 1992.

Howard-Brock, Wes. *Becoming Children of God: John's Gospel and Radical Discipleship*. Maryknoll, NY: Orbis Books, 1994.

———. *John's Gospel & the Renewal of the Church*. Maryknoll, NY: Orbis Books, 1997.

Acts of the Apostles

Cassidy, Richard J. *Society and Politics in the Acts of the Apostles*. Maryknoll, NY: Orbis Books, 1987.

Paul

Elliott, Neil. *Liberating Paul: The Justice of God and the Politics of the Apostle*. Maryknoll, NY: Orbis Books, 1994.

Horsley, Richard A., ed. *Paul and Politics: Ekklesia, Israel, Imperium, Interpretation: Essays in Honor of Krister Stendahl*. Harrisburg, PA: Trinity Press International, 2000.

Haughey, John C. "Eucharist at Corinth," in *Above Every Name: the Lordship of Christ and Social Systems*, ed. by Thomas E. Clarke. Mahwah, NJ: Paulist Press, 1980.

Horrell, David G. *The Social Ethos of the Corinthian Correspondence: From 1 Corinthians to 1 Clement*. Edinburgh: T & T Clark.

Meeks, Wayne A. *The First Urban Christians: The Social World of the Apostle Paul*. 2nd ed. New Haven: Yale University Press, 2003.

Murphy-O'Connor, Jerome. *Paul: A Critical Life*. New York: Oxford University Press, 1996.

Sanders, E. P. *Paul and Palestinian Judaism: A Comparison of Patterns of Religion*. Minneapolis: Fortress Press, 1977.

Commentaries of a More General Character

Borg, Marcus J. *Conflict, Holiness, and Politics in the Teachings of Jesus*. Harrisburg, PA: Trinity Press International, 1998.

Brown, Raymond E. *An Introduction to New Testament Christology*. Mahwah, NJ: Paulist Press, 1994.

Esler, Philip F., ed. *Modeling Early Christianity: Social-scientific Studies of the New Testament in its Context*. London: Routledge, 1995.

Horsley, Richard A. *Archaeology, History, and Society in Galilee: The Social Context of Jesus and the Rabbis*. Harrisburg, PA: Trinity Press International, 1996.

————. *Galilee: History Politics People.* Harrisburg, PA: Trinity Press International, 1995.

Horsley, Richard A., and Neil Asher Silberman. *The Message of the Kingdom: How Jesus and Paul Ignited a Revolution and Transformed the Ancient World.* New York: Grosset/Putnam, 1997.

Lee, Bernard J. *The Galilean Jewishness of Jesus: Retrieving the Jewish Origins of Christianity.* Mahwah, NJ: Paulist Press, 1988.

————. *Jesus and the Metaphors of God: the Christs of the New Testament.* Mahwah, NJ: Paulist Press, 1993.

Malina, Bruce J. and Richard L. Rohrbaugh. *Social-Science Commentary on the Synoptic Gospels.* 2nd ed. Minneapolis: Fortress Press, 2003.

Neusner, Jacob et al., eds. *The Social World of Formative Christianity and Judaism: Essays in Tribute to Howard Clark Kee.* Minneapolis: Fortress Press, 1988.

Reed, Jonathan L. *Archaeology and the Galilean Jesus: a Re-examination of the Evidence.* Harrisburg, PA: Trinity Press International, 2000.

Rohrbaugh, Richard L., ed. *The Social Sciences and New Testament Interpretation.* Peabody, MA: Hendrickson Publishers, 1996.

Theissen, Gerd. *The Gospels in Context: Social and Political History in the Synoptic Tradition.* Translated by Linda M. Maloney. Minneapolis: Fortress Press, 1991.

————. *Sociology of Early Palestinian Christianity.* Translated by John Bowden. Minneapolis: Fortress Press, 1978.

West, Gerald O. *Biblical Hermeneutics of Liberation: Modes of Reading the Bible in the South African Context.* 2nd ed., rev. Maryknoll, NY: Orbis Books, 1995.

FOUR

EUCHARIST: A COMMUNITY'S RITE

I am convinced that Christianity is an explosion waiting to go off, a revolutionary idea still to be comprehended, a banquet in time and history that has barely been nibbled at, and a source of social change the dimensions of which are not even being dreamed of. These potentialities may remain unrealized because of the way we go about Eucharist—what we bring to it, what we bring from it. For that reason I think Christianity's potentiality will move to actuality only if Eucharist is celebrated in a different way and with a different perspective than it ordinarily is today.... [W]e do not need to devise alternative forms of worship ...we need to worship according to the alternative we have become in Christ. (Haughey, 1987, 81-82)

Introduction

I concur with John Haughey's assessment: we need to worship according to the alternative we have become in Christ. We struggle to retrieve some early power of eucharist when the church clearly saw the relationship between the bread as body and themselves as body.

Statements like these, of course, can be romanticized. But our eucharistic imagination should never settle for too little in the matter of a ritual life.

As we know from Paul's first letter to the Corinthians, Paul was clear about the splendor of the Eucharist, and just as clear about the liturgical abuses in that community. It will be instructive to see what conditions made those particular problems even noticeable.

A truly and deeply eucharistic community is hard to find. In Western culture generally and in the US specifically, there is an individualism that makes it difficult to construct the community base which Eucharist presupposes. By that I mean a community that is aware of what the Paschal mystery has done, is doing, and may yet do for it and within it and for the world through it. I mean a community that brings that explicit experience into the Eucharistic celebration of thanksgiving, with ritual drama, and "full, conscious, active participation." Finally, I mean a community that is commissioned anew by its Eucharist to the reign of God in ways specific to its resources and energies. I believe that religious communities are specially positioned as places where communities-in-permanent-mission, with significant shared experience, can best explore, in the name of the entire church, what it means to be a eucharistic community.

At one level, we might explain the ups and downs of eucharistic practice as the ebb and flow between charism and order. As members of religious communities, we have experienced the struggle to both keep the first fire (charism) alive and maintain the structures (order) necessary to interpret it, articulate it, and hand it on. But Haughey is basically correct: rarely do people assemble on the basis of shared experience that united them before they arrived at Eucharist and will keep them united when they go forth, aware that they come to Eucharist as themselves the body of Christ.

The theses of this chapter are twofold. The first is that the recovery of the power of Eucharist in communities of religious life is about the best thing that could happen to us, especially when we connect our deep story to the missioning that happens in every Eucharist. The second is that our religious communities are in fact small church communities, so that our retrieval of eucharistic centrality may be done on behalf of everyone's church.

Over the years there have been multiple Catholic cultural identifiers, from "Catholics don't eat meat on Friday" to "Catholics go to confession" (though not like they used to). Certainly, Mary has a central place in Catholic piety. During the God is Dead movement of the 1960s, one often heard George Santayana quoted, that "God is Dead and Mary is his Mother." Catholics would get the point with a ready grin. But of all the cultural identifiers, surely the most central is that "Catholics go to Mass."

But Mass is in trouble today. In the early 1960s, Catholic Sunday Mass attendance was between seventy-five and eighty percent. In a 1993 study, the attendance rate was twenty-six percent. Gallup has a higher figure, based upon telephone interviews. In the study to which I refer, the research methodology included counting how many people actually showed up on Sunday in comparison with membership on parish rolls (Hadaway, Marler, Chaves, 1993, 741-752). The problem only gets worse as the number of priests decreases rapidly and parishes are combined into mega-parishes. Some thirteen percent of parishes do not have resident pastors, a number that is steadily increasing.

The issue is that Eucharist belongs at the center of a community's life, and whatever best serves that centrality deserves a hearing.

The history of Catholic eucharistic practices and eucharistic interpretations is rich and varied, filled with debate and controversy as well as fundamental agreement and deep satisfaction. There are swings back and forth between merely commemorative interpretations and highly physical interpretations of the body of Christ. And there are swings between a primacy of meal/banquet interpretations with the table at the interpretive center, and a primacy of sacrificial interpretations with the altar at the interpretative center. These emphases are sometimes signaled in language such as "the Lord's Supper" and/or "The Holy Sacrifice of the Mass." Some eucharistic theologies have focused on the eucharistic elements (e.g., transubstantiation) and others upon the eucharist as a liturgical action of a community.

There are tensions built into ritual texture. A particular celebration must not be so generic that the assembled community's life is not reflected. Nor should it be so locally specific that a member of another local church would not be at home.

In the reflections that are central to this chapter, I will focus especially (though not exclusively) on two factors: the first is the importance of the celebrating community as the body of Christ; the second, the relationship of Eucharist to the mission of the community. Every Christian community is both gathered and sent. Every community is a community permanently in mission. A religious community is a celibate community-in-permanent-mission, with mission further specified by its congregational deep story.

A Difficult Time for this Discussion

The sobering decrease in the number of priests for Catholic life cannot but frame a discussion like this. There was a time when women's communities and non-clerical men's communities had their own chaplains. Some men's communities, such as the Sacred Heart Brothers and the Marianists, have a majority of non-ordained members, with priests ordained *mensa communis*, i.e., for the community's life.

This means that many religious communities do not celebrate their own Eucharist, but rather participate in parish eucharistic liturgies, with the result that is often overlooked in the broader scheme. So I will reflect upon some ideal possibilities that remain open to us, aware that we make whatever adaptations our current and local situations require us to make. Another difficulty was perhaps presaged by *Sacrosanctum concilium* itself:

> Even in the liturgy, the Church has no wish to impose a rigid uniformity in matters which do not involve the faith or the good of the whole community. Rather, she respects and fosters the spiritual adornments and gifts of the various races and peoples. Anything in their way that is not indissolubly bound up with superstition and error she studies with sympathy, and, if possible, preserves intact. Sometimes in fact she admits such things into the liturgy itself, as long as they harmonize with its true and authentic spirit. (#37)

This remarkably open invitation seems to allow for great adaptation. But in the following paragraph (#38) a directive insists "that the substantial unity of the Roman rite is [to be] maintained." The Roman rite itself is a particular cultural style that places considerable limitations on what might happen in Kenya, or India, or Japan—or, for that matter, in the United States.

The conciliar document also stresses in a number of places the role of "competent territorial bodies of bishops" in applying these adaptations to local cultures (e.g., #22.2). As I write, a recent document, *Liturgiam authenticam*, puts considerable restraints on bishops, for example, in overseeing the translation of both Scripture and liturgical texts, to best serve particular cultures, insisting on an increasingly literal translation from Latin (not even from the original Greek in the case of the Christian Scriptures, or Hebrew and Greek in the case of the Hebrew Scriptures).

Overview of this Chapter

I will begin with three of the earliest developed reflections on Eucharist: that of Paul in his First Letter to the Corinthians, that of Luke's theology of Eucharist in his narrative of the Emmaus appearance, and that of the eucharistic institution accounts. We will then consult the historical work of liturgist Nathan Mitchell on developments of eucharistic piety beyond the celebration of Eucharist on the Lord's day. There will follow a brief survey of the rich tradition of theological reflection on the Eucharist, after which we will review Louis-Marie Chauvet's and Kenan Osborne's very important recent work on sacrament and liturgy. Finally, we will consider some implications for religious life.

There is no unbiased approach to a topic like this. By bias I mean the presuppositions that we bring to a reflection, the starting points without which reflection cannot even occur. My bias is the reinvention of charism in active, apostolic religious communities, undertaken for the good of the church.

Three New Testament Traditions

A Pauline Tradition

What kind of relationship among those celebrating Eucharist, and between them and Christ, must be presupposed in order to understand what empowers and what debilitates the ritual celebration? And what might the implications for religious communities be? For answers, let us examine the eucharistic practices at Corinth and Emmaus.

Whether there actually was a Last Supper at which Jesus spoke the "words of institution" in the way they are reported has been called into question in some recent biblical scholarship, nevertheless, there is some agreement that the Last Supper is part of a pattern of table fellowship that defined the relationship between Jesus and his disciples.

The four accounts of the meal are not identical in detail, but agree in the ritual elements: Jesus took bread, blessed it, broke it, and gave it to his disciples to eat. The earliest written account of the meal is in Paul's First Letter to the Corinthians. I am inclined to agree with Koenig that Paul's reporting of the meal event lends credence to its actual occurrence as a special instance of table fellowship (Koenig, 2000, 10-14). We cannot date exactly either Paul's persecution of Christians or his conversion experience. But his interaction with the followers of Jesus suggests that his engagement in the Christ event occurred perhaps less than ten years after the death of Jesus. Soon after his conversion, he spent time with Peter and James, and surely his understanding of Eucharist is nourished by what he learned from them, live participants in the Great Meal event.

What we later came to call Eucharist was originally embedded within an actual meal, a custom then still observed in the Corinth of Paul. The breaking of the bread almost certainly took place as the actual breaking of bread which began a meal; and the designation of the cup of the covenant in the blood of Jesus came at the end, "after the meal was finished."

Recall that Paul capitalized upon a social form familiar in the Greco-Roman world, the "household." The household is a recognizable group of people: usually a middle-class houseowner, his immediate family, but also servants, clients, and friends. The household thus included members from different social classes, a distinction not lost on those included, their close interconnections notwithstanding. The members are sufficiently bonded that we hear a number of times that a leader of a household and all the members of that household were baptized. There are people who know each other and who experience their connectedness as a household. Households that are baptized are the early house churches.

The meal/Eucharist combination is clearly reflected in Paul's interaction with the Corinthian community and his chagrin at their meal behaviors:

> Now that I am on the subject of instruction, I cannot congratulate you on the meetings you hold.... I hear that when you meet, there are separate factions among you, and to some extent, I believe it.... So when you meet together, it is not the Lord's supper that you eat; for when the eating begins, each one of you has your own supper first. So then there is one going hungry while another is getting drunk. Surely you have homes for doing your eating and drinking in.... All of you should examine yourselves, and only then eat of the bread and drink from the cup, because those who eat and drink without recognizing the body are eating and drinking their own condemnation.... Now each of you is Christ's body, each of you with a part to play in the whole. (I Cor 11:17, 20-22a, 28-29; 12:27)

At their gathering, they are not behaving towards each other the way the body of Christ should comport itself. Socio-economic factors are subverting appropriate eucharistic behavior. When Paul chides them for not recognizing the body, it is not that they do not recognize the changed reality of the bread as body, but that they do not recognize themselves as body or the essential relationship between their own reality and the reality of the bread.

> Their sin was not a lack of faith in Jesus. It was erroneous judgment. They were in error about who they were because they were in error about who he was now. They conveniently sacramentalized the second part of the evening (Eucharist) after having profaned the first

part (the table fellowship) by inappropriate sociability. (Haughey, 1980, 117, 118)

I agree with Haughey's assessment that our theological tradition has been overly preoccupied with attention to an individuated Christ and too little concerned with what he calls the social flesh of Christ, which so engaged Paul (Haughey, 1980, 108-109). Nathan Mitchell observes the following about the Pauline tradition:

> Paul represents a tradition that stresses the community and its new covenant relationship with the Lord. The meal seals and ratifies this covenant, and in the context of the meal the Lord is experienced as powerfully present "eating and drinking along with his people." (Mitchell, 1982, 26)

What he says of the Pauline tradition is equally true of Luke's Emmaus tradition.

A Lukan Tradition

The narrative of the disciples heading for Emmaus is a Lukan summary of the dynamics of Christian life. In is the bridge between the life of Jesus in the Gospel and the life of the community in Acts. We begin with the text (from Luke 24):

> On that same day two [disciples] were walking towards the village of Emmaus, about seven miles from Jerusalem. They were talking together about all the things that had been happening. While they were walking and talking together about those things, Jesus himself joined them and walked by their side, but their eyes kept them from recognizing him. He said, "What are the events you are talking about as you walk along?" They stopped, and their faces were downcast. One of the two, the one named Cleopas, responded to him, "You must be the only person in Jerusalem who is not aware of the things that have been occurring there the last few days." Jesus asked, "What things?" "All about Jesus of Nazareth," they answered. "He showed himself to be a great prophet, powerful in his action and his speech before God and before all the people. But then our chief priests and our leaders handed him over to a death sentence and they had him crucified. We had hoped that he would be the one to set Israel free.

And this is not the whole story. Two days have passed since these things happened. And some women from our group have astounded us. In the early morning they went to the tomb, and they could not find the body. They returned to tell us that they had seen a vision of angels who told them that he was alive. And some of our other friends went to the tomb, and everything was just as the women had described. But they saw nothing of him."

Then Jesus said, "You foolish people. You are so slow to believe all the things the prophets have said. Was it not necessary that the Messiah had to suffer before he entered his glory?" Then, beginning with Moses, he went through all of the prophets, explaining the passages that were about himself.

When they were close to the village to which they were going, he acted as if he would continue further. But they urged him to stay with them. "It is nearly evening," they said, "the day is almost over." So he went in to stay with them.

Now when he was at table with them, he took bread, said the blessing, broke the bread, and gave it to them. And their eyes were opened. They recognized him. But he had vanished from sight. Then they said to each other, "Were not our hearts burning within us, as he spoke with us on the road and explained the Scriptures to us?"

They set out that very moment, and returned to Jerusalem…They told their story of what had happened on the road, and about how they recognized him in the breaking of the bread.

Two people identified only as followers of Jesus are on the road from Jerusalem to Emmaus, some seven miles distant. Although often pictured in Christian art as two male disciples, the likelihood is that the two people heading home together are husband and wife. In the patriarchal writing of history in Luke's time, it was commonplace regularly to give men's names, but to name women only when they had done something out of the ordinary. We learn that one person's name is Cleopas, a man's name; but the other is unnamed, and is, therefore, almost certainly a woman.

They are discussing the recent events—the news—that happened in Jerusalem. Jesus, whom they are not able to recognize, catches up with them and joins in the conversation and the walk. They tell him what happened, and share their deep disappointment. They describe Jesus as a great prophet, who they had hoped would be the one to set Israel free. They are interpreting the news, and their hopes, aspirations, and disappointments around the news. Jesus then begins to interpret Scripture, and to relate it to the news of the day.

As they near Emmaus, the two disciples invite Jesus to stay for the night, since it is late. A meal is prepared. In the language of eucharistic ritual, Jesus takes bread, blesses it, breaks it, and gives it to them to eat. They recognize Jesus in their midst in the breaking of the bread, and at that point Jesus, who walked and talked with them, disappears from their midst. Immediately they recognize that already while walking and talking about the news and the Scriptures, their hearts were burning within them. One thinks immediately of Karl Barth's characterization of Christians who keep the newspaper in one hand and the Bible in the other.

This new experience of Jesus is such good news that they cannot simply keep it to themselves. It missions them. As late as it is, they set out immediately on the seven-mile walk back to Jerusalem to tell others what they have experienced.

The homiletic function is the connecting of lived experience and Scripture in such a fashion as to show the way to live the Christian experience. When religious communities facilitate the finding of our way through conversation between experience and Scripture, between Word and world, our deep story is a religious resource that belongs with Word because it is an important way in which God continues to speak to us.

It was clear to those of us involved in research on small Christian communities in the US Catholic Church that the dialogue between Scripture and experience was the central empowering and rewarding experience. These groups, which average thirteen adult members, are small enough that all regularly present take an active part in the homiletic conversation. Sometimes the naming of experience is more local and personal, and sometimes it is more communal and about the wider world. The Emmaus metaphor of walking and talking along the way is apt. It does more than just lead us to "fulfill our Sunday obligation." It leads us to hunger for the Eucharist of the Lord's Day, to both need and want it. What happens to people who share a history on the way to Eucharist is critical to what happens to those same people at the Eucharist. When the effective meeting of Word and world causes our hearts to burn within us on the way to Table, we are best prepared to meet Christ in the breaking of the bread. A meeting with Christ, like a meeting with anyone, is not simply a matter of being "there."

Meeting is dialogic. It depends on what both bring to the encounter. In the case of Eucharist, this means not just what individuals bring to the encounter one by one, but what a community brings in its communal heart. The density of presence may be fierce or negligible. Great presence is the congruence of the gift offered by God and the gift received by us with responsive awareness of how our reception implicates us. A regular prayer pattern that engages Word, world, and our community's deep story is, by Lukan logic, about the best thing we can do to give Eucharist the defining power that Catholic culture knows it can have.

The "Institution" Tradition

That theology is "diachronic" means that it cuts a wide swath through the centuries. If you ask "what is church," the full richness of the response includes what church means in Matthew's gospel (the only gospel where the word *ekklesia* is found), what is means before and after Constantine, before and after the Reformation, before and after Vatican I, before and after Vatican II, and so on. It is important not to read later interpretations back into early interpretations. I am interested in loosening up the theology of Eucharist for the sake of its richness, and am suggesting that religious communities are in a privileged position to recover, not only for their own sake but also on behalf of church, a much wider and deeper appropriation of eucharistic life.

In Greek and Latin, as in most modern romance languages, gender does not necessarily name a male or female or a thing (neuter). Adjectives, like nouns, have gender, and the gender of the adjective agrees with the gender of the noun. Pronouns work that way too, as do demonstratives like "this" and "that" and "these" and "those." In Greek the word for bread is *artos*, and it is a masculine noun. If I want the word "this" to refer specifically to the bread in Greek, the word would be *houtos*. So when Jesus takes the bread and says "This is my body," we would expect to see the Greek word *houtos*. But instead, the word is *touto*, the neuter form, which suggests a wider applicability.

Jesus takes bread and then speaks, so certainly the bread is included in the *touto*/this; but, perhaps, so is the assembled community, for in a Pauline sense the community is likewise the body of Christ. Now Jesus spoke Aramaic, so we do not have his exact words. But the Greek interpretation of the experience seems to say grammatically that the "this" in "this is my body" obviously indicates the bread but also includes something wider than the bread, and that would surely seem to be the gathered community. The becomings that happen to the eucharistic elements and to the eucharistic community are of a piece.

The Complexity of Eucharistic History

In his recent book, *Christian Sacraments in a Postmodern World*, Kenan Osborne remarks that "contemporary sacramental theology for the first time in the entire history of the Christian Catholic Church has a scholarly grasp of the history of the ritual sacraments"; and he notes that "there is a clear dialectic between the historical data and the Christian doctrine on the sacraments" (Osborne, 1999, 45, 46).

The historical scholarship of the twentieth century has brought to fruition an interest in scientific historiography that takes shape as early as the late eighteenth century with Samuel Reimaurus' *The Aims of Jesus and the Disciples*, which started the quest for the historical Jesus. Any college student today who has taken a course in the sacraments understands more about the varied interpretations and concrete expressions of them than did Thomas Aquinas when he wrote his treatises on the sacraments for the *Summa Theologica*.

As we learn more about the history of the Church, sacraments, and liturgy, we recognize a very wide range of interpretations and practices. I am mindful of a remark of Cardinal Ratzinger cited by Cardinal Kasper in their recent discussion about church. In the context of ecumenism, Cardinal Ratzinger referred to some of the earlier harmonious ways in which the role of the Bishop of Rome was understood in relation to patriarchs in other parts of the church. Perhaps an agreeable working arrangement from the past could work now; we should be open to the possibility.

I want to say something similar about Eucharist. There are multiple theologies of Eucharist, many ritual forms and interpretations, many devotional practices concerning the Blessed Sacrament. If any of them that served the Church well in the past could do so again, we should consider them viable options today. Similarly, as new insights and ritual practices evolved in the past, there will surely be new insights and practices again—new possibilities that do not yet have a history, but may create a history.

Historical Instances

In the very early church, Eucharist was above all a community celebration on the Lord's Day. Justin Martyr and Hippolytus both attest to this practice. A century later, the practice begins to develop (especially in North Africa) of celebrating Eucharist to honor martyrs. Mitchell also cites Augustine's report that Eucharist was celebrated at his mother's graveside at her burial:

> Lo, when her body was carried away, we went out, and we returned without tears. Not even in those prayers we poured forth to you when the sacrifice of our redemption was offered up in her behalf, with the corpse already placed beside the grave before being lowered into it, as is the custom in that place, not even during those prayers did I shed a tear. (Mitchell, 1982, 31)

Early on, the eucharistic bread is reserved for the sick, and taken to them outside of the Eucharist when they are unable to attend. There is also an early practice of taking bread from the Sunday Eucharist into the home for consumption during the week. The eucharistic food achieves some independence outside of the Eucharist, yet it is not until the Carolingian period that we begin to find any extra-liturgical cult of the Eucharist (Mitchell, 1982, 66-67).

I would like to focus on two related concerns: who presides at Eucharist, and the sense of Eucharist as an action of the community. The New Testament never identifies clearly who presides at Eucharist. Vatican II's central biblical commission twice sent a *relatio* (memo) to the bishops working on the Church document to the effect that in the early Church whoever was the leader of a community then also presided over that community's Eucharist.

> Since already in the New Testament and in the post-apostolic era the Eucharist is known as sacrifice, and since the leaders of a community are leaders of Eucharist, the ministerial priesthood of the New Testament shows its own proper dignity from being instituted by Christ. The function of community leader appears to be conjoined with the cultic function.

A Christian community is by nature a eucharistic community, so it makes sense that whoever leads the community also speaks to God with and in the name of the community. A prayer leader can truly pray the prayers of the community only through consistent, active participation in the life of that community. That is how the leader knows and feels and articulates the community's mind and heart. Then, when the leader prays, the community recognizes that its prayers to God are being prayed and voices its recognition through its "Amen," which signals approval.

But somehow the presider became separated from the community. Once Latin was no longer a vernacular, the presider spoke in a language that the community did not understand. It is impossible for a community to experience liturgy as its action when it does not understand the liturgical language. Latin became a clerical language, foreign to the community. Chauvet, citing Heidegger, remarks that "to name things is not just, is not first of all, to attach a label to them for communication. To name is to 'call' things to 'come and be present,' so that they can speak to us" (Chauvet, 2001, 78). That mode of presence does not occur when the naming and calling are in a tongue foreign to those who pronounce the words.

The validity of a sacrament depends on God, which is what *ex opere operato* meant; but a sacrament's fecundity depends on the believing subjects (Chauvet, 2001, 124). The use of a foreign language limits what the believing subjects can experience, and distances them from the action and the presider.

Of much interest today is the renewed practice of taking communion in the hands, which was the custom in the early church. From the early Middle Ages, only the priests with specially consecrated hands could touch the eucharistic elements. A ninth-century council of bishops in Rouen declared, "Let not the Eucharist be put into the hand of any lay man or woman, but only in the mouth" (Chauvet, 2001, 87). When only the priest could touch the eucharistic elements with his hands, the message was clear: it is largely the priest's ritual. Priests, not the community, "said Mass," or "offered Mass."

There is some recent backtracking in *Liturgiam authenticam*, which directs the presider to receive the eucharistic elements before any lay eucharistic ministers even approach the altar table. The document further indicates that the communion vessels are to be purified by the priest, not the lay ministers. Lay people with better learning in Scripture and theology than the parish priests are not allowed to give the homily at Mass, although lay preaching clearly has a history in the Catholic Church.

If the liturgy is to function once again truly and palpably as an action of the people as the body of Christ, some major adjustments need to be made. Whatever has been a helpful and valid manner of ecclesial experience anywhere in our history can be recalled.

Back to the Future

Back to the Future is the name of a well-known movie with Michael J. Fox. The title might well apply to liturgical renewal; the Rite of Christian Initiation is a stellar example. Every initiation happens to a community, not just in a community and not just for the person being initiated. The community is responsible for the socialization of a catechumen into the life of Christ and the life of the Church. Every sacrament is in some critical way an act of the whole Christ in the celebrating community.

In renovations of church buildings, the issue of whether or not the communion rail should be removed caused many a pitched battle. The space on one side of the communion rail has traditionally been interpreted as sacred, and is called the sanctuary. It is the territory of the priest and altar servers. The space where "the people" are located is considered profane, or at least far less sacred. The communion rail was a highly charged symbol because it was thought to demarcate sacred and profane space. The fact that Eucharist "happened" in the sacred space made it very difficult to perceive the liturgy as an action of the community, albeit in union with the bishop and with a recognized community elder necessarily presiding. The Greek word *presbyteros* means, in fact, an elder.

Canon law reflects the *Catechism's* affirmation that liturgy is an action of the whole community (#1140): "Liturgical actions are not private actions but celebrations of the Church itself, which is the 'sacrament of unity,' namely, a holy people, assembled and ordered under the bishop" (Canon #837). What we want to recover is a deep understanding from the past (some pasts shouldn't be reclaimed) that liturgy is an action of the people of God, presupposing God's initiative for its validity and the community's responsiveness for its fecundity. This, of course, is everyone's quest. It is the quest of religious communities because they belong to the "everyone."

Liturgy as the Action of a Community

In Matthew 16:18, Jesus says "You are Peter, and upon the rock I will build my church." The translation used in the New Jerusalem Bible has Jesus say, "You are Peter, and upon this rock I will build my community." The New Jerusalem Bible's editorial note on the verse says that the Greek word *ekklesia* probably renders the Hebrew word *qahal*, which means "an assembly called together." The English word "community" conveys that sense more clearly, because it is difficult to hear the word "church" without thinking about the institution that came into existence later, but did not exist as such in Jesus' time.

The emphasis is not only on community as the liturgical subject, but on the fact that liturgy is community action.

One of the major characteristics of rituality is surely that it aims at being *operative*. In contrast to scientific discourse, which pertains to "-logy," that is, structured discourse (biology, sociology, musicology, theology, and so on), the liturgy pertains to "-urgy," a term that comes from the Greek *ergon*, designating precisely "action" or "work," in contradistinction to logos. Terms like "metallurgy" and "chemurgy" designate an activity, a work. However, liturgical action belongs to the symbolic not the technical order: it aims at establishing communication between the participants and God and as a consequence among themselves. (Chauvet, 2001, 99)

I would substitute "conversation" for "communication." The ritual promotes a conversation between the participants and God and, as a consequence, conversation among the participants themselves. Conversation and conversion are two English words made from identical Latin roots. There is truth to the observation that one cannot exit from a true conversation exactly the same as one entered the conversation. True conversation is never just talking. And transformation is the nature of the liturgical action.

Since the early medieval period, the liturgical tradition has tended to focus its attention on interpreting the transformation of the eucharistic elements. And since the high Middle Ages, the transformation of the elements has been expressed through the concept of transubstantiation. In the eucharistic ritual, the bread and the cup of wine become something other than what they were before the ritual.

In both formal theology and in popular devotion, the efficient causality (what makes it happen) of the transformation has been identified with the consecratory words of the priest over the eucharistic elements, further isolating the eucharistic transformation of elements from the transformation of the community more fully into the body of Christ. But the deeper eucharistic tradition tells a different story which is reflected in the Catechism.

The eucharistic presider regularly prays through "we" and not merely as "I." The presider says the prayers of the community in the name of the community. In the epiclesis, "the priest begs the Father to send the Holy Spirit, the Sanctifier, so that the offerings may become the body and blood of Christ ..." (*Catechism*, #1105). It is our faith that when the priest prays the community's prayer, the Holy Spirit acts. The *Catechism* approvingly cites St. John Damascene:

> You ask how the bread becomes the Body of Christ, and the wine...the Blood of Christ. I shall tell you: the Holy Spirit comes upon them and accomplishes what surpasses every word and thought...(*Catechism*, 1106)

Article #1105 on the Epiclesis says that the Holy Spirit transforms the elements, and "that the faithful, by receiving them, may themselves become a living offering to God." The community is also transformed. Reflecting further on the epiclesis, we hear that God sends the Spirit to makes people's lives (like the bread and wine) into a living sacrifice "through their spiritual transformation into the image of Christ...by taking part in [the church's] mission through the witness and service of charity" (#1109). The mission of the community receives specific definition from the Liturgy of the Word so that the faithful and the ministers "can live out the meaning of what they hear, contemplate, and do in the celebration" (#1101).

The transforming work of the Holy Spirit, therefore, acts on the elements ("especially in the eucharistic species" #1088), the community, and the world through the community missioned in Eucharist. The eucharistic liturgy is, therefore, not merely an action of the community but a transformational action of the community.

What does this mean?

As I have previously indicated, everything said so far is not specific to religious life, but applies to every Catholic and every Eucharist. I believe, however, that communities of religious are in a particularly good position to help the church return to eucharist as an action of the community in conversation with the action of God, because we are an interactive community outside of and before and after the eucharistic ritual moments. If we make Word and Eucharist utterly central and defining, our religious exercises will take on some new configurations for us, and can enrich the church's recovery of liturgy as an action of a community within the universal ecclesial community. I will speak to this under two topics: rhythm and scale.

Rhythm

I would propose for consideration, for example, that Eucharist may be served well by reserving it for the Lord's Day and other truly major feasts. I would include eucharistic observances that belong to a religious community's deep story (but in moderation so that the church cycle does not get drowned). I do not mean that every or any religious community should go this way, although that idea merits consideration.

The practice of daily Eucharist has a long, noble, and continuing history. John Foley's rationale for it is stated clearly and convincingly in *Review for Religious* (Foley, 2001, 342-364), and I recommend his presentation. The theo-logic is sound. But it is not the only sound option, as the Church's earlier practice testifies.

I offer three reasons for considering a more restricted practice. First of all, the careful preparation that liturgy deserves is truly time consuming. The selection of music alone is challenging. Thomas Day's book, *Why Catholics Can't Sing*, is a sound commentary on music. Preparing the liturgy of the Word requires, often with some urgency if the texts are complex, some research among good scriptural commentaries. To find an effective mix of any good liturgy's repetitive and universal elements with the community's local life taxes any celebrating community's resources.

Second, a community's adequate preparation of itself for Eucharist also takes time. Assessing a community's present experience as Word's dialogic partner requires not just a homilist's attention, but also that of the community. The reflective time of the heart and mind before Eucharist, and the processing time during and after Eucharist require focused, deliberate commitment.

God's validating presence is always there. The community's work (the –urgy of liturgy) has a profound effect upon the Eucharist's fecundity. Or, to recall an earlier motif, the issue is not presence/absence, but the density of presence (another way of describing fecundity). Presence is whatever has a hold on a community's becoming, and on an individual's becoming as a member of that community.

Third, and perhaps the most controversial point, daily Eucharist runs the risk of turning Eucharist into a devotion more than a ritual with the gathered community as the liturgical subject. Repetitive elements are essential to every effective ritual, but repetition can also trivialize. Devotion is indeed fitting for Eucharist, but above all, it is a community action.

In my Marianist history there is an interesting section on the community's religious practices in the first Constitution for the Society of Mary, approved in 1839:

> Mental prayer is the common and unique source of all the virtues...If, by reason of indisposition or pressing affairs and while traveling, a member is obliged to suppress a part of his customary exercises, he retains mental prayer in preference to all that is not of precept, such as Mass on Sunday or the Breviary for priests.

We have not followed this directive in our time.

I would consider the encounter with God's presence, by an individual or a community, in dialogue with lived experience to be a contemporary form of mental prayer. A community can make mental prayer (meditation) together as well as engage in mental prayer as individual prayer. I understand easily (and experientially) how anticipating the Eucharist of the Lord's Day is nourished by meditation, and how remembering it in the week following inserts itself into meditation.

Scale

I want to note the importance of what might be called "scale" in church life. Paul is able to recognize the failings of the Corinthian community because the scale was small enough for their behaviors towards each other to be clearly noted, so that both their successes and failures as a house church are quite visible. If Paul scolds the house church at Corinth, he also sometimes praises these early communities for their fidelity. Something very important characterizes the celebration of the Eucharist when the assembly is a group of people who share some significant memories and hope—namely, they have some experiential awareness of themselves as the body of Christ.

It is important that the gathered community is small enough for its relational behaviors to be visible and nameable. If for the most part the only gathering of a parish community is the Sunday Eucharist, the small scale that operates in Corinth cannot happen. This dimension of ecclesial life is being brought back into focus by small Christian communities throughout the world.

How large, then, is a small group, a small community? The dynamic of a small group starts with five. Five is not just one more than four, but represents a different dynamic. If two or three are gathered in Jesus' name, Jesus is there. But that is not the issue. The issue is what promotes a healthy interactional dynamic that has the feel of a group. At the other end, twelve is about the limit if regular interaction between all of the community members is an ideal. If there are more than twelve, the group can be divided into smaller segments which report in to the whole community.

I am currently in a house church community with more than twelve. We look after our community life under three headings: our inner life (*missio ad intra*), our public life (*missio ad extra*), and all of the practicalities that concern our community life (calendars, communications, and so on). Every member of the community belongs to one of these three committees. The three committees do not assume responsibility for the activities in each of these three areas, but for animating the entire house church in each of these areas.

A Christian community that is the body of Christ is also and always a social system. What affects the whole affects all the parts; and the condition of any part has effects upon the whole. Paul is clear about this, especially in chapter 12 of the First Letter to the Corinthians. This interrelatedness presupposes a pattern of interaction and mutual presence, and creates a sense of the Christian calling at odds with American individualism.

In the United States, parish assemblies are rarely that kind of a group. A parish is a geographically defined entity. Geographical closeness was once a natural form of community (and perhaps still is in a few rural areas), but this is not the case in modern urban and suburban life. The exceptions, and they are recent, are parishes that follow something akin to the models being developed by the National Alliance of Parishes Restructuring into Communities.

Religious communities are often the kind of group that can enrich the texture of any eucharistic assembly, if the intention is there. We know each other. We share a life. We participate in a common history. For us, for example, the kiss of peace can be a very awkward moment when we know that alienation exists, as in the Corinthian community; or it can be a powerful positive moment for those who know they are the body.

Ecclesiologically, it is not enough to be only a small community. We are church with every other community and with the universal church. But if the small building blocks are not reasonably strong and secure, neither is the whole Church. And the small building blocks are basically communities that assemble, not individuals who come one by one without mutual relationships with others who assemble. This is when scale shows its importance. And this is why the eucharistic practices of religious communities have a great gift to offer the church today. We often have the scale and the community life. We do not, however, always have an awareness that it is our body-of-Christ reality that justifies our Eucharists. We are not there, ought not to be there, as solitary individuals without relation to the whole body.

When Christians travel or visit, we still belong even in a new place where we do not have existential relationships, for our baptism has long since joined our destinies. But in our own local churches we are called to be there as community.

The Churchhood of Religious Communities?

Paul sometimes spoke about the church at someone's house, the early House Church. He also sometimes addressed the church at Corinth, where there were multiple house churches. Churchhood applied to both the small community and the community of communities. The small Christian communities throughout the world have a growing sense that churchhood is theirs too.

Four descriptors of church are: *koinonia*, the inner life of community and its connection to the larger ecclesial community; *diakonia*, the ministry through which a community serves to the larger world; *kerygma*, the grounding of its life in the Good News of Jesus Christ;

and *leitourgia*, a ritual life that church knows and practices, usually liturgy of the Word in the small Christian communities. These do not "constitute" churchhood, much less exhaust the idea. But wherever there is church, these are found. The self-perception of themselves as small churches has led the Latin American communities to add the word ecclesial to their naming: basic ecclesial communities. The language for small Christian communities in the US Catholic Church is beginning to shift similarly to "small church communities."

Though never separated from the hierarchical structure, religious communities do have something of a parallel structure. Religious communities regularly had their own established chapels. Some men's communities still have ordained members and non-ordained members. Women's and men's nonclerical communities often had their own chaplains. In these arrangements there is a kind of recognition of the churchhood of communities of religious. It may be helpful to us today, as we grow and define ourselves in new ways, to think of our individual communities as small churches, deeply influenced by the community's deep story, on the way to becoming charism for the Church.

Let us conclude with three reflections on liturgy. The first is from one of Christianity's early testimonies about eucharistic practice, that of Justin Martyr (mid-second century), the second from a contemporary writer, Annie Dillard, the third from Alfred North Whitehead:

At the conclusion of the prayers we greet one another with a kiss. Then bread and a cup containing wine and water are presented to the one presiding over the brothers [and sisters]. He takes them and offers praise and glory to the Father of all, through the name of the Son and of the Holy Spirit, and he makes a lengthy thanksgiving to God because he has counted us worthy of such favors. At the end of these prayers and thanksgiving, all express their consent by saying "Amen." This Hebrew word, Amen, means "So be it." And when the one who presides has given thanks, and all the people have acclaimed their consent, those whom we call deacons summon each one present to partake of the bread and wine and water over which the thanksgiving was said, and they carry it to those who are absent. We call this food "Eucharist," literally "Thanksgiving." No one is allowed to partake of it except one who believes that our teachings are true and has been cleansed in the bath for forgiveness of sins and for regeneration, and who lives as Christ commanded. Not as common bread and drink do we receive these, but just as through the word of God, Jesus Christ, our Savior, became incarnate and took on flesh and blood for our salvation, so, we have been taught, the food over which thanks has been given by the prayer of his word, and which nourishes our flesh and blood by assimilation, is both the flesh and blood of that incarnate Jesus. (*First Apology*)

Here is Annie Dillard's poetic and rousing exhortation never to minimize the power of worship:

Does anyone have the foggiest idea what sort of power we so blithely invoke?...We should be wearing crash helmets. Ushers should issue life preservers and signal flares; they should lash us to the pews, for the sleeping god may awake some day and take offense, or the waking god may draw us out to where we can never return. (Dillard, 1982, 41-42)

And lastly, from the concluding paragraph of Whitehead's *Science and the Modern World:*

The power of God is the worship [God] inspires. That religion is strong which in its ritual and its modes of thought evokes an apprehension of the commanding vision. The worship of God is not a rule of safety—it is an adventure of the spirit, a flight after the unattainable. The death of religion comes with the repression of the high hope of adventure. (Whitehead, 1925, 268-269)

FOR DISCUSSION

1. One of the toughest challenges to building the power of Eucharist is for the celebrating community to have consciously shared community experience, and to recognize how that experience gathers them to the Table. What kinds of living promote that kind of eucharistic celebration? What kinds of things get in the way?

2. A related and equally challenging issue is the connection between effective community leadership and eucharistic presiding. Identity some of the concrete issues around this issue, and ways to address them.

3. What are your preferences about the rhythm of eucharistic celebrations: daily? Sunday and feasts? And for what reasons?

FIVE

A GODLY WORLD AND A WORLDLY GOD

Introduction

This book's subtitle indicates that it is an essay in worldly spirituality. Worldly spirituality is no different for members of active, apostolic religious congregations than it is for lay Catholics, except that celibate community is the context in which members of religious communities live the mission of Jesus Christ.

It is true to say that in the minds of most people "worldly" and "spiritual" are irreconcilable. Indeed, there are perhaps gnostic tendencies in the fourth gospel, intimations that the world is not good, and the writings of Augustine are suffused with Manichaean dualism.

Worldly spirituality is not naive about the ambiguity of the world. As Paul said, "sin abounds." But he followed that with the judgment that "grace superabounds." Sometimes the margin is very small indeed. Yet in the creation narrative in Genesis, God looks at all that God has made and judges that: "It is good." Even so, the fall of angels and that of human beings is not far distant.

While there is no pure analogical or dialectical imagination about these things, David Tracy holds that the Protestant imagination tends to be dialectic, emphasizing the deep differences between the creator and creation, whereas the Catholic imagination tends to value the ways in which creation images the creator. "The world," says the Catholic poet Gerald Manley Hopkins, "is charged with the grandeur of God." Catholicism's powerful fascination with and experience of the sacramentality of the world presupposes an analogical imagination.

In a March 4th entry to his existentialist diary, *Being and Having*, Catholic philosopher Gabriel Marcel criticizes a spirituality which views creation negatively and tries to get around it instead of through it.

> My deepest and most unshakable conviction—and if it is heretical, so much the worse for orthodoxy—is, that whatever all the thinkers and doctors have said, it is not God's will at all to be loved by us against the Creation, but rather glorified through the Creation and with Creation as our starting point. That is why I find so many devotional books intolerable. The God who is set up against the Creation and who is somehow jealous of his own works is, to my mind, nothing but an idol. It is a relief to me to have written this. (Marcel, 1965, 135)

This book presumes that Creation is our starting point. It is where we are.

There are four reflections on world in this chapter. The first reflection is indebted to process theology, and will address the relationship between immanence and transcendence. There is no path to transcendence except through worldly immanence. The second reflection is deeply indebted to the extraordinary work of Bernard Cooke, especially his analysis of the distancing of God and the need for a recovery of the world's sacramentality (with an important qualification on sacramentality from the work of Kenan Osborne). I want to suggest that there is no unmediated experience of God, which is a variation of the dictum that there is no uninterpreted experience.

The third reflection concerns theological anthropology and constitutes a thesis which is central to this book—namely, that being human means performing thoughtful action in the world. In some ways this discussion will continue the previous one, for the same paradigm responsible for the distancing of God is also responsible for elevating the contemplative life over the active life. The thought of the Scottish philosopher John Macmurray and the German philosopher Hannah Arendt will be helpful on this point.

To address mission as a shape of Christian action, in the fourth reflection, I will rely on the Hebrew word *dabhar* to establish an action or, better, an enactment context. The religious celibate community is a community-in-mission. This is a Hebrew anthropology which I believe would have been understandable to Jesus.

The Worldly Appearances of God:
Immanence and Transcendence

We are in the world in and through and with our bodies. We are bodied. There is nothing we can know that does not originate in experience (personal, communal, vicarious). We can reason further, based upon experience, and with imagination triggered by experience.

If empirical means grounded in concrete experience (which is far broader than quantitative and qualitative scientific research), then we are talking empiricism. Experience, however, is far broader than sense experience. We do not know through sense experience directly how profoundly language or culture, for example, accounts for what we see and what we don't see. We rarely are aware of how the deep story, in which we come to consciousness, has a narrative structure in which our grasp of morality is founded. In some quarters, "empirical" appears hostile to religion. I concur with William James, however, that if experience is understood in the broadest sense, then empiricism is religion's best ally. It keeps us grounded. And "ground" is a good metaphor in this case. Adam—humanity—comes from the Hebrew word for ground.

If the human experience of God is truly possible, then it must be the case that God is in the world with us in some fashion. Perhaps minimally, God is in the world in the way that every artisan is present in every artifact. Or maximally, God is in the world through the "speech" of God and the "action" of God.

I often have recourse to Martin Buber's reflection that people often wonder why God doesn't speak as much today as God is said to have spoken earlier. Buber says the problem is ours because we do not know where to listen, expecting the speech of God to occur above everyday life, or alongside it, rather than within and through it. All the events that call us to decision, he says, are in fact empowered by the personal speech of God. If we do not hear God speak, he continues, it is because we ourselves have put wax in our ears.

The kind of listening it takes to hear new words of God is not easy. Doing it well requires right habits that are long in the making. Consciousness is highly selective. Whatever age we are, the accumulated experience of infancy, childhood, youth, young adulthood, middle age, old age (with both its wisdom and its forgetfulness) affects what we see and do not see, and how we value and evaluate what we experience. Our language and culture do the same thing. Consciousness is always very selective. There are depths of every experience that are never reached. In hermeneutics we sometimes refer to the surplus of meaning that attends all experience. Whitehead writes,

> Consciousness flickers; and even at its brightest there is a small focal region of clear illumination and a large penumbral region of experience which tells of intense experience [but] in dim apprehension. The simplicity of clear consciousness is no measure of the complexity of complete experience. (Whitehead, 1978, 267)

Events have their origin in long historical chains of causality and their unpredictable effects continue on and on and on. Bernard Meland says that "whether one is speaking of some happening, a person, an institution, the living community, or of God, one is dealing with an inexhaustible event, the fullness of which bursts every definitive category" (Meland, 1953, 64). When we sense that we are not hearing the word of God, in all probability we are not listening with the habits of reflection and discipline that are needed. Meland names two attitudes needed for listening at the depth at which God might be speaking. There must be a complete relinquishment of vested interests, and a readiness to be broken in upon by the new experience. The act of feeling into a situation or into an object, the full meaning of which one cannot grasp, is an important aspect of cognition itself (ibid., 64, 65).

I like the expression "religious practices," because cultivating necessary listening habits requires lots and lots of practice, as Meland's remarks indicate. Listening to meanings behind the text, within the text, and in front of the text (for its first writers, readers, and hearers) requires practice and discipline. And listening to events, as well as texts, is no easy matter. Somewhere in between plain old common sense readings of events and scholarly research are the readings that come from the wise practitioners. If God speaks to us through experience, it takes long practiced listening; or we, like the people of whom Buber writes, will wonder why God is no longer speaking.

Rahner observes that all human experience of God is mediated: through events, through language and culture, through history, through tradition, through sacraments, and so forth:

> Therefore turning toward history is not something optional for us. Because of our specific human spirituality, it is always already basically imposed on us. Detaching [*Loslosung*] ourselves consciously from our history would put us in intrinsic contradiction with our own nature, not simply insofar as the later possesses a biological aspect, but with regard to its spiritual aspect....Thus the place of a possible revelation is always and necessarily our history. (Rahner, 1994 [1940], 137-138, 94)

Martin Buber adds some clarification: "We expect a theophany of which we know nothing but the place, and the place is called community" (Buber, 1966, 117).

Henry Nelson Wieman, another process theologian, stresses that reflective time is needed for assimilation and integration of experience. He speaks of individual reflective processing, but I believe that communities also need time alone and apart:

> When many meanings have been acquired through communication and through much action on the material world, there must be time for these to be assimilated. If one does not draw apart... the ceaseless stream of new meanings will prevent deeper integration.... (Wieman, 1967, 60)

Although I do not agree with Wieman's identification of God with what he calls the creative good, I recognize the urging of God towards the increase in good in the world, for which "reign of God" is a root metaphor. The assimilation of new meanings and new modes is seldom without pain or without loneliness, which is why the prophets did not welcome their prophetic vocation. Jeremiah's rage and pain are dramatically poignant. In religious life we like to think of our shared life as prophetic (as we should), but that does not make community life easy.

Advances in the community experience are not necessarily pleasant; the good produced by the creative event brings an increase in suffering as well as intense joy; community brings a burden as well as a release. Those who cannot endure suffering cannot endure the increase of human good. Refusal to accept suffering is perhaps the chief obstacle to increasing the good of human existence (Wieman, 1967, 65).

Buber is right about community being a locus of theophany, and community is never an easy achievement.

I hope it is clear that when I speak of a worldly spirituality I am fully aware of the danger of romanticizing the world. While its goodness is the ontological reason for sacramentality, it never loses its ambiguity, or its deep darkness and its abiding resistance to goodness. To Augustinian "original sin," or Matthew Fox's "original blessing," I prefer the term "original ambiguity," which belongs to the nature of finitude. But there is a tilt towards grace.

If the world mediates our experience of God, i.e., if the world is a sacrament of God (*sacramentum mundi*), by the same token it mediates God's redemptive initiatives in human history. God's intentions for the world are God's gift to the world. And God requires human collaboration for their realization. Wieman, cited just above, says that how all of this works has been his life-long study:

> What operates in human life with such character and power that it will transform us as we cannot transform ourselves, saving us from evil and leading us to the best that human life can ever reach, provided we meet the required conditions? One of the required conditions is faith. Religious faith is giving ourselves in the wholeness of our being, so far as we are able, to what we believe has the character

and power just mentioned...Transformation can occur only in the form of events...Nothing can transform us unless it actually operates in human life. Therefore, in human life, if the actual processes of human existence, must be found the saving and transforming power which religious inquiry seeks and which faith must apprehend. (Wieman, 1969, 3-4)

It takes eyes of faith to discern the work of grace in the internal and external dynamics of relationships and events.

Because we are in the world, and only there, and there in an irreducibly bodied way, we can only know God if God is immanent in the world. The expression "totally other" is poetically powerful as an expression of the grandeur of God, but it cannot be metaphysical. Anything that is truly totally other cannot be experienced. While we do experience God in the world, we never experience the fullness of God, the greatness of God, the extraordinary power of God. God transcends our experience of God's immanence, which we can only dimly perceive. However, the only transcendence that we can apprehend is that which is triggered by our experience of God's immanence.

When I first know someone, I may often be puzzled by what that person does or says or means. There is a lot of unknown. As I get to know the person better, more and more of that unknown falls away. But I never know all there is to know, not even about myself. Not all the words one has ever spoken or all the actions one has ever done fully disclose who one is. Each person transcends all that he or she says and does, and our only hints at that unplumbed richness of identity are housed in immanence.

It is remarkable when someone that I have known long and well takes me utterly by surprise by some unexpected action or remark. The profoundest experience of transcendence is not just the natural mystery of someone's otherness and unfamiliarity. The great experiences of transcendence are routed directly through immanence. The unknown and puzzling should not be mistaken for transcendence. Immanence and transcendence are coordinate experiences. Our experience of God's immanence begins always and only in our worldly experience of God, for our experience of God is in the world. We are only in the world and nowhere else. God's being in the world with us is where we start.

I want to be clear about my emphasis upon the immanence of God in the world as the basis of our experience of God. We need to find the places where, as Bernard Meland sometimes put it, "Ultimacy traffics with immediacy even as it forever transcends immediacy."

There is an analogy with human relationships. When I first meet someone, that person's otherness may seem very great because my experience of that person is so limited. But after years and years of friendship and love, when a lot of knowing has transpired, I am most in touch with the otherness of another, nourished now by the depth of experience, when the mystery of otherness is so palpable. The subjectivity of an "other" outruns all our knowing. The otherness remains always, and transcends a lifetime of tender knowing, and is all the more clear when the best knowing in the world has only approached the otherness of the "other." It would be a deeply flawed relationship if familiarity appeared to conquer the unknown and unknowable rather that deepen it. The better we know God, the more radiant and perpetually elusive is God's otherness. But immanence is the only "where" from which we set out.

God: How Near or How Far?

I passed through eight years in a parish grade school, four years in a Catholic high school, and four years in a Catholic university, taking religion courses all the while, without ever having opened a Bible. Much of the language I learned about God, especially in the university, was abstract and philosophical: God is immutable (cannot change), impassible (cannot suffer), ineffable (can only be described through the negation of limitation), omniscient (knows all the past, present, and future), omnipotent (unlimited in absolute power), and so forth.

In a course in natural theology I learned that these adjectives were necessary deductions from the logic of perfection. If a being could be better tomorrow than today, it is not perfect; or worse tomorrow than today, still not perfect; or even just different tomorrow than today, still not perfect because that being is not today all that it can be. Perfect being, therefore, cannot change or suffer any limitation. Since new knowledge would effect change, God must know the future perfectly.

During a course in Old Testament, I learned how differently the Hebrews named God. In the first place, there is such a reverence that writing out or pronouncing the name of God is not done. In print today, for example, we often just see YHWH. Some letters are omitted. But the most amazing thing was that God is described by worldly events, rather than in logical and philosophical terms: God who made the world, and the sun and stars and moon; the God of Abraham, Isaac, and Jacob; God who leads us out of slavery in Egypt; God who leads us across the Reed Sea; God who helps David beat Goliath; God who promises a land of milk and honey. All these names are rooted in some past worldly phenomenon, or some expected historical event where YHWH's action is experienced or anticipated. The starting points are God's historical immanence, experienced or expected. God is always more than God's historical immanence, and greater than all our experiences of God's immanence, but our knowledge of him arises from his interventions in history.

In Jeremiah 18:7–12, YHWH names either the punishment or reward intended for God's people, but notes that depending on how his people respond, YHWH will then behave accordingly: "I then change my mind." Jesus tells a parable in Luke 18:1–8. A widow wants justice and a judge keeps refusing to grant her petition. But the widow pesters him until the judge finally does her bidding: "I must give the widow her just rights since she keeps pestering me, or she will come and slap me in the face." One possible conclusion for us is to pester God, presuming that this will have effects not otherwise forthcoming. Both of these stories presume that God can change his mind. So "immutable" isn't applicable.

The Western Christian tradition is so profoundly influenced by Aristotelian and scholastic philosophy that it discounts as anthropomorphisms the Hebrew (and New Testament) suggestions that God changes in response to free human actions. One way of appreciating the difference is to remember that the Greek rational interpretation is founded upon the logic of perfect being, while the Hebrew experiential interpretation is founded upon the logic of perfect love. Perfect love is always vulnerable and responsive to the actions of the beloved. In that logic, God would not be immutable but the ultimate in loving mutability.

What both affirm is the perfection of God, and each does it in the logic of its presuppositions about reality.

Jews at prayer bring the prayer shawl over their heads (if using one), sway back and forth, and whisper in an undertone. At the wailing wall, the movement of praying Jews is relentless. This in sharp contrast to the Western Christian prayer model, which is still and quiet. There is more than just a contrast of prayer attitudes here. It is a difference of very basic narrative structures, i.e., deep stories.

We all have some "basic logic," of which we are seldom conscious. Some call it a worldview; for others, it is simply a set of presuppositions about reality. It is never possible to know any system of thought well until one knows a contrasting system of thought really well. That is when we get substantial hints about what we have presupposed without knowing it.

My own encounter with process philosophy put me in touch with the world of scholastic thought in which my faith was reared and in which the faith of Western Christianity has been reared. By this I mean that Greek thought, especially Platonism, Neo-Platonism, Stoicism, and Aristotelian thought, provided a framework for the evolution of Christian doctrine.

All of this might seem far-fetched in a book on religious life. But our assumptive worlds world have an immense impact upon how we understand God and humanity, and upon how religious experience occurs. I believe that God honors our assumptive worlds (except in their aberrations) and comes into our experience through them. Our assumptive worlds provide for us both the scope and limitations of how and what we experience. In other words, our assumptive worlds provide the symbolic structure through which sacramentality operates.

I am deeply indebted to the work of Bernard Cooke in his book, *The Distancing of God: The Ambiguity of Symbol in History and Theology.* He focuses "throughout on symbols' role either in making God present to humans or in distancing God from human consciousness" (Cooke, 1990, 6). Cooke is singularly attentive to the contrast between the assumptive world of Jesus and the Greek world view.

The Jewish assumptive world presumes that God and the world are naturally interrelated and mutually experiencing each other. This assumptive world would never articulate a metaphysical distinction between natural and supernatural. God is not, however, thereby trimmed down to human size. God excels above all, and is nonetheless always here among us. The nearness of God never jeopardizes the grandeur of God, nor is the grandeur ever minimalized. This people's statements about God, therefore, include the historical references to their concrete experience of God. "I am the God who brought your ancestors out of Egypt" (Jer 31:32).

In contrast to this Jewish understanding of the world and of God, the Greek understanding of the world presumes a metaphysical divide between creation and creator. Philo, an Alexandrian Jew and a contemporary of Jesus, developed a hellenized system of Jewish thinking. He was a profoundly committed Jew, who came up with Greek explanations for all of his Jewishness. In so doing he modified how the relationship between God and the world is understood and lived out. Philo sees God as so totally other that creatures cannot experience God. However, he proposed a theory for how that total otherness can be apprehended.

When God chose to create the world, he did so through the Logos, which came from God from all eternity. The Logos comprises all of God's ideas about what a world might look like, and when the world is created, every created thing is an instance of one of God's ideas, i.e., his Logos. The Logos mediates God's presence in the world and gives us access to God. Without the Logos of God, we could never experience God. To experience God, we must transcend our sense experience of everything (Philo regarded senses as the lower mind). Only when we get near the pure idea do we begin to make contact with the Logos in the very nature of things; then we know something actual about God.

There is an unbridgeable gap between the sensible world and God, a great, great distance, but Logos bridges the chasm. This interpretation of reality, in effect, distances our fundamental sensibilities from our immediate contact with the world

The Jewish world did not take up the Philonic interpretative option, but Christian thought did do so. Bernard Cooke observes:

> In doctrine and formal theology...it was the Greek influence that soon dominated the developing understanding of faith as the convergence of divine and human activity in the process of salvation... Faith came to be seen less as a commitment that involves the entire person and more as a process of human thought probing divine mystery, less as ministering discipleship and more as contemplation. (Cooke, 1990, 42)

In some key ways, the difference between Hebrew and Greek presuppositions about the world and God reflects the soteriological difference between the synoptic gospels and the fourth gospel. In the synoptics, there is a decided tilt to the call to a "ministering discipleship." The disciples, with Jesus, face God and the demands that the reign of God makes upon them. In the fourth gospel, the followers fix their gaze upon Jesus, which is phenomenologically interchangeable with a focus upon God. This I see as a difference that arises from the underlying assumptive worlds between the two traditions.

The point of this reflection is the nearness of God and God's accessibility in everyday life and experience. Again, as Cooke points out, "experience" doesn't mean that in our conscious awareness we accurately mirror the prestructured outside world (Cooke, 1990, 349). Knowledge does not just mirror the reality outside it. Interpretation is always a factor. We see what our assumptive world sets us up to see. We feel what our traditions and past experience set us up to feel. To meet God in immediate lived experience requires an expectation that it is possible. The world is not simply and immediately a sacrament of God's presence, as Kenan Osborne's recent book on sacraments states:

> Sacramental *haecceitas* [a particular instance] occurs when a human person or human persons begin to react to the blessing *qua* blessing of God in the tree, in the cloud, or in the river...There is not an objective world, unaffected by subjectivity, which one can call sacra-

ment. Only divine action and human reaction in a concrete situation form the basis for possible sacramentality. Sacramentality is possible whenever God acts and there is also a subsequent human response to this action of God. Only in such a dual dimension is the sacramentality of the world possible and meaningful. (Osborne, 1999, 75, 74)

One of the reasons I have stressed liturgy of the Word so strongly is that in the form often used in small Christian communities it requires a conversation between faith and experience. I have also encouraged religious communities to bring their congregation's deep story into the dialogue. It should be one of the major formative factors of our assumptive world, determining how and where the sacramentality of the world makes God present to and for us, and what it requires of us. The same set of circumstances addressed by two different religious communities in the context of the same biblical text will mediate the speech of God differently because their deep stories shape what they behold and how they respond. The deep story frames the sacramentality of God in a religious community's lived experience.

The Active Religious Apostolic Person

The reflection in this section of the chapter is about the meaning of "person." Tell just about any Western people that you pray for them that they may know their most special gifts and become the unique individuals that God wants them to be, and they will say "Thank you." But if you say the same thing to Buddhists, they will want to know why you have such ill will toward them, for the striving for individual fulfillment and uniqueness is the source of unhappiness. What truly makes a Western Christian happy and what truly makes a Buddhist happy differ because the underlying anthropologies are so different. But in each case, the meaning of "person" mediates their human experience, their becoming, and their genuine religious fulfillment.

As I began writing this chapter, I received in the mail a new book, by a friend and colleague, Hugh Bihl, SM, which is one volume in an international series on modern theology and Marianist spirituality. The book is entitled *The Marianist Person at the Dawn of the Twenty-First*

Century. Bihl begins with documents from the founding period (early nineteenth century, in the aftermath of the French Revolution) and cites developments along the way up to the present period. I will cite some of the texts. Although the language will differ from that of other community histories, underlying anthropological similarities will be apparent.

"Soul" language is commonplace. We become religious to save our own souls and "for the salvation of souls." We were asked "to renounce oneself totally, no longer want to judge anything by one's own mind, or to do anything by one's own choice." For the religious "there is no longer anything beautiful or curious to see, no longer any pleasure to be found in creatures, no longer any amusements, frivolous conversations or correspondence, no longer any pleasure trips or amusing reading, no longer any consolations other than those it pleases God to bestow by his grace for the sacrifices of virtue." A good religious has "renounced the world and all it contains …News and affairs on earth no longer interest him."

At the end of the nineteenth century, childhood images appear as an interpretative model for a Marianist religious. We are children of God. We are attentive to the maternal care of Mary in raising Jesus, and our apostolic attitudes reflect that. We are especially attentive to Jesus' filial piety towards Mary. Briefly, this is a much gentler assessment of human experience, though not without problems in today's world, such as paternalism.

Profound changes occurred in the wake of Vatican II. We are to confront history, not avoid it. We are to love and appreciate the world, though always critically. We align ourselves with God's commitments to mercy and justice. We are responsible for the poor. We are deliberately in the world, part of the world, responsive to the world. The Marianist, like every human being, "is seeking and longing for freedom within an authentic human community; he is searching for freedom from evil, ignorance, poverty, oppression, division, and hatred in all forms. He is hoping for someone or something to liberate him from uneasiness about the present and from apprehension about the future and to create for him a place in community. He would be free to understand, to love, and to act—in a word, to be fully alive, to have life and have it more abundantly."

There has been a very deep anthropological shift in the Christian understanding of the nature of the human person and, correspondingly, in the relation of a Christian to the world. The Jesuit anthropologist, Pierre Teilhard de Chardin, was one of the early proponents of this shift. He understood the transformation of historical existence as part of the Incarnation, making the world become Christ's body:

> By virtue of the Creation, and still more, of the Incarnation, nothing here below is profane for those who know how to see. On the contrary, everything is sacred to those who can distinguish that portion of chosen being which is subject to Christ's drawing power in the process of consummation...If your work enthralls you, then allow the spiritual impulse which matter communicates to you to enter into your taste for God whom you know better and desire more under the veil of his works. (Teilhard de Chardin, 1965, 66)

This understanding of the Christian person opens up the sacramentality of the world.

The French editor of *Le Milieu Divin* includes some writings of Teilhard that were not part of the original text. Among them is a reflection on his priesthood:

> To the full extent of my power, because I am a priest, I wish from now on to be the first to become conscious of all that the world loves, pursues, and suffers; I want to be the first to seek, to sympathize and to suffer; the first to open myself out and sacrifice myself— to become more widely human and more nobly of the earth than any of the world's servants. (Teilhard de Chardin, 1965, 105)

There are clear resonances with the familiar opening passage of *Gaudium et Spes*.

Peter Berger (and others who write about the sociology of knowledge) say that it is difficult to find some universally agreed upon definition of "human nature," other than the fact that it is a human calling to define the meaning of "person." This is a social construction of reality (Berger, 1969, 7). What person means and how persons are

expected to function are rooted in any culture's deep story, or founding narrative.

What It Means to be Human: Two Models

Anthropology is the exploration of what it means to lead a human life
in a particular culture at a particular time. Every theology, like every
culture, has some anthropological underpinnings, not always consciously acknowledged. We will look at two contrasting models, each
of which grounds religious life differently.

I want to compare the sense of person that Christianity inherited
from Greek culture with an alternative anthropology that has been
taking shape in the modern Western world. It is a contrast between
seeing reason or rationality as the key to personhood vs. historical
agency as the key. These two views are not diametrically opposed, and
there are elements of both in each of the two approaches I will
describe. But where the priorities come down is an issue of great and
deep practical import.

I am proposing that many aspects of person as historical agent are
congenial to American instincts, and also supportive of the vocation of
active, apostolic religious congregations. My point is not that one is better than other, but that both are usable, and one is perhaps especially
suited to the American world in which we live today. I find it interesting
that these anthropological avenues have opened up in the non-
Romance cultures—Great Britain, Germany, as well as the United
States—where the Greco-Roman hold on sensibilities is less pronounced.

In an earlier part of this chapter, I contrasted two fundamental attitudes towards the world, one of which requires some distancing from
the world in view of the nature of Creator and creation, the other of
which encourages a critical but unreserved worldly plunge. These are
contrasting tendencies. The discussion that follows builds upon these
same tendencies, but the perspective shifts.

The Contemplator

We are all familiar with the way in which spirituality has long valued
contemplation over action, which the story of Mary and Martha has
often wrongly been used to support. In fact Mary was not contemplat-

ing. She was in an animated conversation with Jesus. In the Platonic/Stoic construction of reality, all created things are imperfect instances of a perfect idea, which is in the mind of God. When we use our reason to understand the nature of something, i.e., the idea which it instances albeit imperfectly, and if we can abstract from the creature and focus on the idea, we draw near to God. In this abstracting distancing from individual, particular, and always imperfect creatures, we learn to contemplate the ideal and, in so doing, we draw nearer to God. Our rational abilities enable us to do this, and when we do, our nature is fulfilled.

In Aristotle's paradigm, there are three kinds of knowledge. The highest and most perfect is the knowledge and contemplation of truth, beauty, and goodness. It is in this contemplative possession of theoretical knowledge (his name for it), arrived at through the exercise of human reason, that a human person finds perfect fulfillment, for that is what we are meant to do as persons.

The next kind of knowledge is knowing what kind of a world we should be working to achieve, and knowing how to go about doing so. In fact, the knowing and doing continually shape each other. Knowing clarifies what needs to be done, and action nourishes the knowing. It is circular. For Aristotle it is a close call whether this kind of knowledge and the acting in which it implicates us is an intellectual virtue (knowing) or a moral virtue (acting as one should). What is clear is that one cannot be a virtuous person if one knows what kind of a world we should be enacting but then does not get involved in bringing it about. He considers politics to be a virtue connected with this kind of knowledge (which he calls *phronesis*), because actually enacting a world that clearly should be enacted requires an abundance of discussion, tact, and compromise.

At the bottom of the list, though absolutely necessary for human life, is the knowledge of how to make things and the art and skill needed actually to make them: a house, a chair, a bowl, a barrel of wine, a good cheese, a flower arrangement. This he calls technique (*techne*).

Phronesis is where we locate the human person as an historical agent, but for Aristotle (and the tradition influenced by his assessment), *phronesis/praxis* is a lesser kind of knowing compared with theoretical knowledge and contemplation. Today most of us understand theory to be insight into the natures of things, and as such it serves our being in the world. But theory, for Aristotle, is only the contemplation of perfect truth, beauty, and goodness; it has no practical payoff. He says, for example, that the theoretical knowledge possessed by two very famous wise people, Anaxagoras and Thales, is "remarkable, admirable, difficult, and divine, but useless [as far as practical things go]."

Our human splendor lies in our reason, and our happiness in reason's finest fulfillment, contemplation. The notion of beatific vision, the contemplation of God, is an essential part of this anthropology.

This emphasis on the primacy of reason makes orthodoxy (accurate conceptualization of truth) more important than orthopraxy (right behavior). Modernists like George Tyrrell and Alfred Loisy were excommunicated for their writings. Pierre Teilhard de Chardin was not allowed to publish in the area of religious thought. At different times Yves Congar, Henri de Lubac, Karl Rahner, Piet Schoonenberg, Edward Schillebeeckx have been under suspicion. All of these were in trouble because of their thinking. Two other Catholics, Adolph Hitler and Benito Mussolini, were not excommunicated for their acting.

How we think about reality, especially the realities of our faith, is critically important. There is no question about that. But I have wanted to indicate priorities generated by the anthropology that have, in great measure, supported the emergence of the Western Christian tradition, in both doctrine and spirituality. This anthropology (not so much a single system but a family of related world views) has effectively mediated our religious experience of God and our understanding of Christian existence in the Western Christian tradition. The lives of many saints reflect this spiritual model.

The Historical Agent

The anthropology of person as historical agent has much in the tradition to support it. It both harks back to a Hebrew sense of person and looks forward as a contemporary Western sense of person. The tension between contemplation and action becomes more of a restless rhythm between the two, like a balance between Aristotle's notion of *phronesis* as a kind of knowledge and *praxis* as its lived expression.

Person Acting

In this part of the chapter we will look at three principal resources: the Gifford lectures of John Macmurray; Alfred North Whitehead's book, *The Function of Reason*, and Hannah Arendt's book, *The Human Condition*.

John Macmurray

> What is here proposed is that we should substitute the "I do" for the "I think" as our starting point and center of reference; and do our thinking from the standpoint of action....We must not underestimate the difficulty of the enterprise to which we are committed...To change our standpoint is to transform habits of thought. It is not to change one theory for another, but to change the basis of all theory. (Macmurray, 1991, 84, 85)

This chapter presents not so much a different theory about religious life, but a change in the foundation of most theories. It proposes deep transformation of the symbolic structure in which our self-understanding is embedded. It is not a matter of changing one's way of thinking to better accommodate the active life, but because it is also a way of interpreting the meaning of person and community that resonates with our culture as well as with many of the social constructions of human reality that would have been part of the assumptive world of Jesus.

The Gifford lectures are perhaps the most prestigious lectureship in the humanities in the Western world and include, for example, Alfred North Whitehead's *Process and Reality*, William James' *Varieties of Religious Experience*, and Gabriel Marcel's *The Mystery of Being*. John Macmurray, a Scottish philosopher, gave the Gifford lectures in 1953 ("The Self as Agent") and 1954 ("Persons in Community"). Macmurray, who had a great influence on the thinking of the present British Prime Minister, Tony Blair, is less known in the United States than in the United Kingdom. I believe that this work can help those of us in active religious congregations authentically retell our deep story in the idiom of our cultural world.

Macmurray notes at the start that "the Self that reflects and the Self that acts is the same Self," but he insists that "action and thought are contrasted modes of its activity" (Macmurray 1991, 86). That we do our thinking from the standpoint of action contrasts with the other presupposition that we do (or should do) our acting from the standpoint of thinking. Subsequent traditions of practical theology insist on the ceaseless rhythm between thinking and acting that continually nourishes and revises them both.

> Action…is a full concrete activity of the self in which all our capacities are employed; while thought is constituted by the exclusion of some of our powers and a withdrawal into an activity which is less concrete and less complete. (ibid.)

For the thinking activity, the critical categories are "true" and "false." For the action activity, the basic categories are "right" and "wrong" (or "good" and "bad" or "evil"). In a philosophical anthropology which focuses upon the self as agent, right and wrong are of primary importance:

> If the concept of "pure thought" is derived from the concept of action by exclusion, then thought, so far as it is actual, falls within action and depends upon action. Action is primary and concrete, thought is secondary, abstract, and derivative. This must mean that the distinction between "right" and "wrong," which is constitutive for action, is the primary standard of validity; while the distinction between "true" and "false" is secondary. (Macmurray, 1978, 89)

Truth is no less important for the actor than for the contemplator, but priorities change in ways that touch upon the whole pattern of living.

Alfred North Whitehead

In his book, *The Function of Reason*, Alfred North Whitehead comes to a similar conclusion. He proposes that reason develops in human life over a long period of time in order to address three challenges: to live (i.e., to survive), to live well (i.e, to live more comfortably), and finally to live better (to use imagination and analytical skills to construct social systems that help people expand their capabilities and develop loving relationships). For Whitehead, the development of what we call human rationality occurred with the social evolution of the human species.

Hannah Arendt

Like John Macmurray, Hannah Arendt makes an important distinction between activity and action. Three kinds of activity take place in human life. The first of these is labor, which embraces those fundamental things people must do simply to meet the basic needs that insure survival. "The human condition of labor is life itself" (Arendt, 1958, 7). The second kind of activity is work, which for her is the activity of making things. We make things that enrich living, make it easier and more enjoyable. We can and do also make things that are dangerous and destructive. Arts and skills belong to work.

The third kind of activity, upon which her book focuses, is action. She bases the necessity of action on three factors: natality, mortality, and plurality. I will focus on the last of these three.

Plurality is the condition of human action because we are all the same, that is, human, in such a way that nobody is ever the same as anyone else who ever lived, lives, or will live (Arendt, 1958, 8).

Action means to "set something in motion (which is the original meaning of the Latin *agere*)" (Arendt, 1958, 177). Action is a response to our irreducibly social nature, and it is political in character—in the richest sense of "political," which means everything that touches upon how people are together in the world, making it work together. There is no more basic question than "What kind of world do we want to make together for ourselves and our progeny?" That is the nature of the active life, the *vita activa*. Being Christian means that we accept the revelation of God in Jesus Christ concerning God's intentions for the world. That is the heart of Christian discipleship, the *vita activa Christiana*.

Arendt notes two characteristics of historical reality that require the actions of forgiveness and fidelity to promises. The first is the irreversibility of the past. Redemption from the predicament of irreversibility requires the act of forgiveness (Arendt, 1958, 237).

Forgiveness is the only way of breaking the hold over the past, of allowing a new beginning, a starting over.

The other characteristic of historical reality is its unpredictability. There are no utterly predictable eventualities. The future is shot through and through with historical contingency. "The remedy for unpredictability," says Arendt, "for the chaotic uncertainty of the future, is contained in the faculty to make and keep promises" (Arendt, 1958, 237). Contracts, covenants, agreements, promises give the future some degree of manageability, some stability. They make planning possible.

Our biblical destiny is to be holy in the same way that God is holy. Jeremiah connects both historical forgiveness and historical fidelity to the holiness of God who says about his people: "They will know me from the least to the greatest...since I shall forgive their guilt and never more call their sins to mind" (Jer 31:34). Real forgiveness means that I will no longer "remember" your guilt, i.e., I will not ever bring it up again and let it condition our future relations. YHWH's fidelity is in the promise: "I have loved you with an everlasting love, so faithful am I in my affection for you" (Jer 32:3).

The Matthean community was so clear about the consequences of irreversibility that it understood that God's forgiveness of us is dependent upon our forgiveness of one another (chapter 6), and even puts into the mouth of Jesus a manual for conflict resolution (chapter 18). Fidelity is clear in Paul's assertion that Jesus is an unqualified Yes to God, and is our model.

These, then, are essential dimensions of the activity component of the vita activa: labor, work, and action. It is principally on the sense of action that I focus here, for that is where we work together to set into motion the kind of world we think we should make.

Arendt posits an integral connection between speech and action, both being required for "sheer human togetherness" (Arendt, 1958, 180). We become who we are and we reveal who we are through speech and action. The Hebrew sense of our experience of God is quite similar: we learn who God is through his speaking and acting. Our only access to the Who of God is through God's self-revelation, mediated by God's speaking and acting.

"Signs" are so important in the fourth gospel because they bring the christological meaning of Jesus out into the light. Making a dramatic historical appearance, out in the open for all to behold (grandiose, as it were), is what the Greek word for "glory" means (the Greek *doxa* is related to the verb which means "appearing" or "coming out into the open"):

> Because of its inherent tendency to disclose the agent together with the act, action needs for its full appearance the shining brightness we once called glory, and which is possible only in the public realm. (Arendt, 1958, 180)

Hannah Arendt, John Macmurray, and Alfred North Whitehead all offer an anthropological understanding of the human person with historical action as key, treating thinking from the perspecting of acting.

In the introduction to his book, *Marxism in the Twentieth Century*, the French Marxist Roger Garaudy suggests that why Marxism has such appeal is that it held that history is open-ended, that it is the human task to direct history, and that we are all called to take control of the process of development. While that may be overly optimistic about how much control we have, it does understand that historical agency is the human destiny, and it appeals to many in the modern and post-modern world who share that intuition. The deeper recovery of an active eschatology in Latin American theology may have received a nudge from its dialogue with Marxist thought.

In his book *History and Eschatology*, Rudolph Bultmann suggested that we think of the *eschaton* not as extra-historical or end-time historical, but as the reign of God which Jesus describes in many ways (the Matthean "sermon on the mount" is a good summary). Whenever we incorporate a reign of God ingredient into a present moment, there is genuine *eschaton* in that moment. Bultmann caught the spirit of this:

> Always in your present moment lies the meaning of history, and you cannot see it as a spectator, but only in your responsible decisions. In every moment there slumbers the possibility of being the eschatological moment. You must awaken it. (Bultmann, 1957, 155)

That is another way of speaking about action when a Christian is consciously crafting a new historical moment.

Dabhar and Speech-Action

In the fourth reflection of this chapter I want to return briefly to the Hebrew word *dabhar*, already discussed in the chapter on Word, and to the assumptive world which it presupposes and which would have belonged to Jesus' own world view.

In English, a word is a sound (for which there are also written signs) that stands for some idea in my mind, often an idea of something outside my mind. In ancient Hebrew, however, *dabhar* means a speaking that enacts what it says, and what it brings into being can also be a *dabhar* thing, for *dabhar* can mean "a thing." In other words, *dabhar* can mean a speech-act (enacted speech), or a word-deed (word that gets a thing done), or a word-thing (something brought into existence by speech-act). Speaking belongs to action and action to speaking. In Hebrew thought a lie would consist of speech that does other than what it says; or speech that enacts bad things; or insincere speech that does not follow through. None of these is a true *dabhar* word. Religious conversation is a dialogue of truthful human speech-acts with the speech-acts of God.

It is clear then that there is a great difference between the Hebrew understanding of word and that of Western culture. These are two very different ways of making meaning, and of experiencing reality.

Likewise, there are differences in how our assumptive worlds mediate God's intercourse with us and ours with God. I use the term "intercourse" because it means conversation. But in Hebrew the same word, *yada*, means both sexual intercourse and knowledge. Deep understanding/knowledge is never merely cognitive; it comes from intimate and dialogic interchange. It also draws us into the experience of the transcendence of the other.

A Long Night's Journey into Day?

Parsing the grammar of anthropology can seem like a tedious undertaking as a basis for reflecting on the future and the spirituality of active, apostolic religious congregations. We in the Western Christian tradition have for a long time presupposed the superiority of the contemplative life over the active life, but without awareness of the assumptive world in which that judgment is grounded. Active, apostolic religious life is rescued from second-class citizenship in the modern and postmodern assumptive world in which to be human is to have the vocation of "historical agent," and to be a Christian is to collaborate with God in the realization of God's loving and redemptive intentions for human history. Hannah Arendt observed that

> Perhaps the most momentous of the spiritual consequences of the discoveries of the modern age...has been the reversal of the hierarchical order between the *vita contemplativa* and the *vita activa*. (Arendt, 1958, 289)

The contemplative experience, the quiet, profound, and sometimes ecstatic beholding of the "other," and especially "the Other," is not any less important, but it is important in a different setting.

In any friendship or loving relationship between spouses there is the possibility, the rare moment, of simply beholding each other in profound union. If it happens, it is a defining relational moment. Such moments are arrived at only through a long, sensitive, profoundly mutual history of shared living—through some sort of shared destiny supported by a pattern of committed action and committed speaking together. Insight, understanding, and appreciation grow. The ecstatic moment comes as sheer gift. It cannot be achieved by any direct willing. It lasts briefly, but one sees and knows the world differently in its lasting wake. For the shared acting and speaking on the other side of this experience are forever enriched and transformed.

That gift can only occur through a life of action and speech that is shared; it cannot be willed into existence. The most that two people can do is live in a way that gives such a moment its best chance of being bestowed. The words "discipline" and "asceticism" may seem inappropriate here, but they belong to living in the way that opens us the possibility of ecstasy, whether the relationship has religious connotations or not.

We do not live for the purpose of having those moments. We live, with speaking and acting. Those freely occurring moments belong to a pattern of speaking and acting. The moment itself is a special kind of activity. And the speaking and acting of life go on once again. I am suggesting that the contemplative experience of God is not different. In this anthropology, the *vita contemplativa* is located within the *vita activa*—neither higher nor lower, but a most extraordinary moment of created grace within it. No one "sees" God like that without a lifetime of living that makes it possible.

Reflecting on Luke 10:38–42, I like to think that perhaps Martha and Mary are not two different people, but personifications of the two sides of every person. Martha's action is creating a precious meal time together, and Mary is enjoying conversation with Jesus. The gospel never suggests that it is a contemplative moment, just a great and important conversation. The account in the fourth gospel balances the picture (Jn 11:1–44). It is Martha who runs out to meet Jesus when he arrives. "Mary remained sitting in the house" (Jn 10:20). It is Martha, in this narrative, who engages in extended dialogue with Jesus.

In the course of the conversation, Martha makes the same confession of faith which in Matthew, Mark, and Luke is made only by Peter: "Yes, Lord, I believe that you are the Christ, the Son of God, the one who was to come into the world" (Jn 10:27). Her acting and speaking facilitate that marvelous moment of recognizing that which is deepest and truest about Jesus. Then Martha sends for Mary who comes outside, throws herself at Jesus' feet, and begins a conversation with him (Jn10:28-33).

The active, apostolic life of religious congregations is served by a spirituality which embraces the world, albeit critically, as a "place of God." Jesus is the action and the speech of God to the world about us and about the world. Paul tells us that "all things are yours, you are Christ's, and Christ is God's." Paul is clear as well that if all things are ours, they are meant to be ours only in every way that is consistent with the action and speech of God to us in Jesus Christ. That is Teilhard's meaning when he insists that any increase we can cause in the world is an increase on Christ's hold on the world. He means "increase" that is consistent with God's intentions for the world.

Rainer Maria Rilke's "Ninth Duino Elegy" is an extended reflection on human finitude and our relationship with the world, in keeping with who God is. He asks that we praise the world to God, because we know it and can tell about it, and not be concerned about the untellable, whatever that might be. Because

> ...you can't impress him with the splendor you've felt; in the cosmos
> where he more feelingly feels you're only a novice. So show him
> some simple thing, refashioned by age after age,
> till it lives in our hands and eyes as a part of ourselves.
> Tell him things....
> Show him how happy a thing can be, how guileless and ours.
> What is your urgent command, if not transformation?
> Earth, you darling, I will....Supernumerous existence wells up in my
> heart.

Rilke recognizes that the world needs to be transformed, and he embraces the challenge (Rilke, 1977 [1957], 91-92).

What most insures the right relationship with the world on the part of active, apostolic congregations, is a right relationship with those places in the world where suffering and deprivation are deepest and most resistant to healing and reconciliation. Because we are the body of Christ, we can find Christ in any person. And those most in pain are Christ-like in a way that demands immediate attention. But we should not find Christ in them by identifying with their suffering and pain, but by identifying with everything in them that wants the pain and suffering to cease. That, above all, is the call to action and speaking from active, apostolic religious congregations.

FOR DISCUSSION

1. What are some of the ways a community's spirituality can both passionately embrace the world and not be "conned" by it?

2. Embedded in the Judeo-Christian tradition is the inclination to name God in connection with historical figures and events

through which God's presence was experienced: the God of Abraham (and Sarah}, Isaac (and Rebecca), Jacob (and Rachel); God who led us out of Egypt; etc. How would you complete the phrase, "God who..." based upon your community's history? based upon your personal life experience?

3. Presuppositions about what it means to be human shape our spirituality, like the "contemplator" anthropology and the "history-maker" anthropology. Given the fact that the contemplator really must act and that the history-maker had better contemplate, what differences does it make to see one as the starting point rather than the other?

SIX

COMMUNITY-IN-PERMANENT-MISSION

Introduction

In this chapter I will consider community from several perspectives. The first perspective is that of the social nature of Christian life. Religious in active, apostolic communities choose to express our community apostolically, that is, to offer our know-how about community to the church and to the socio-cultural world in which we live, where community is increasingly at risk.

This would be a straightforward matter if community meant largely similar things to most people. But the word has significantly different meanings from culture to culture, and many variations within the same culture. What the word means for most Americans is conditioned by the emphasis of individualism in our cultural world. In ancient Hebrew culture, "community" was part of the understanding of Covenant, which was central to the people's perception of its relationship to YHWH.

This meaning undergoes a transformation in the powerful preaching of Paul to early followers of Jesus, for he has roots in the Jewish world and in the Greco-Roman world: his father is a Roman citizen (and thus he is too) and his teacher is the renowned Pharisee Gamaliel.

My aim is to illuminate the many facets of "community" which stem from this Covenant inheritance: from Jesus' proclamation of the in-breaking reign of God to the church's recently articulated understanding that God saves us not one by one but as a people; from both problems and possibilities inherent in American culture to the life of active, apostolic communities and their underlying once and future deep stories.

The call to discipleship is deeply personal and foundationally social. "Deeply personal" is at one and the same time "foundationally social." Those called to follow Jesus become immediately connected with others following Jesus. The following of Jesus, by its nature, connects the followers with one another.

One of the great gifts to the church of fifteen hundred years of religious life is an appreciation of community. "Community" belongs to the core of Catholic culture. It is surely part of the Catholic deep story, and belongs to the rhetoric of Catholic culture, e.g., in the ways that "common good" grounds the Catholic ethos. Religious life is a place where the radically social nature of Christian existence is reflected.

There are many reasons for the downturn in regular Sunday Mass attendance; but among them must surely be the diminished sense of community that tends to bring people together. This is not a matter of Catholics "not caring"; rather, the devaluation of "community" in the wider culture is having an effect on us. The analogy is sometimes made that we are not aware of our absolute dependence on air and water unless something happens to it. Culture is like that. We are seldom aware of how we reflect it in our own values and behavior.

In this chapter on community, we will first review the irreducibly social nature of Christian experience, with attention to two theological anthropologies and their respective effects on our understanding of community.

We will then move to a more in-depth discussion of cultural forces in American life, especially as they relate to the experiences of community. Pope Paul VI introduced the notion of the evangelization of culture into Catholic thought. Religious communities should consider how our commitment to community might help the Catholic world evangelize US culture. It will be important to understand the effects of postmodernity on the interpretation and experience of community. This is not a time to be timid about a task that is so daunting. It is time for a bracing dose of eschatology.

In the final part of this chapter we will ponder the challenge of community specifically with respect to religious life. With respect to community, life in front of us will have many different configurations than life behind us.

Community and Covenant

Corporate Personality

When Joshua leads Israel against Ai, against all expectations Israel loses badly. YHWH tells Joshua the reason: "Israel has sinned. They have violated the covenant..." As it turns out, one man, Achan, took unlawful loot, which YHWH had forbidden. As punishment Achan is to be stoned. The illicit booty is brought out from Achan's tent and laid before Joshua and all the Israelites. Achan is taken outside the city to be stoned, along with his sons, daughters, oxen, sheep, donkeys, and goats. All Israel goes outside the town for the stoning, and all Israel stones him.

This may sound primitive to us today. But the profoundly relational sense that underpins the event in the notion that YHWH's covenant is with his people, and the destiny of each member of the people is linked with the entire group, just as the destiny of the people is linked with each member. As I indicated in *Jesus and the Metaphors of God*,

> The relation of individuals to YHWH is mediated through the corporate personality of the nation. The relation of YHWH to individuals is mediated through the corporate personality of the nation (Lee, 1993, 62).

Individuals are important, but it is the individual's relationship to a covenanted nation that makes them so important. When Jesus gives his inaugural address in Luke, he reads from Isaiah 61:

The Spirit of the Lord is upon me, for he has anointed me to bring good news to the afflicted. He has sent me to proclaim liberty to captives, sight to the blind, to let the oppressed go free, to proclaim a year of favor from the Lord. (Lk 4:18–19)

All of those things happen because there is a year of favor from YHWH for YHWH's people. In his study of Jesus and community, Gerhard Lohfink says that "the leaping of the lame and the singing of the dumb are an integral part of Israel's eschatological restoration" (Lohfink, 1982, 13).

The cures that Jesus works often inspire us to be healing presences in the lives of others. And while that is, of course, an entirely valid and generous response, it does not catch either the sense of God's Covenant with a people through Jesus, nor the eschatological promise.

We do not really grasp Jesus' cures, which include the healing of those then considered possessed, if we understand them solely as miracles performed for individuals out of sympathy for their illness. Since the eschatological horizon of Jesus' activity has reentered consciousness, it has been clear that Jesus' miracles of healing must be seen in connection with his preaching of the kingdom of God....When the kingdom of God arrived, sickness simply had to disappear....Inseparable from the eschatological horizon of Jesus' miracles is their relationship to community; they served the restoration of the people of God, among whom, in the eschatological age of salvation, no disease is permitted. (Lohfink, 1982, 12-13, passim)

The multiplication of the loaves and fishes to feed crowds and the miracle of the wedding feast at Cana are certainly evocative of the picture drawn by Isaiah of the new world that YHWH will create for all peoples:

On this mountain, for all peoples,
YHWH Sabaoth is preparing
a banquet of rich food,
a banquet of fine wines,
of succulent food,
of well-strained wines....

The Lord YHWH has wiped away
the tears from every cheek.
YHWH has taken YHWH's people's shame
everywhere on earth,
for YHWH has spoken. (Is 25:6,8)

Recall that at Cana the head waiter marvels that the groom has kept the best wine till last. In a word, the reign of God happens to a people, God's people—and to me and you because we belong to that people.

Community and Households

Paul's community-founding activity takes place in the Hellenistic world. Covenant and corporate personality are not working parts of that culture. But there is a social form that has some significance for our understanding of community: the household. "Household" includes not only the kin-related people who live in the same house, but also clients, servants, slaves, and business connections. It is a voluntary association, but one with an identity and a definite membership.

We get some idea of the cohesiveness of the group from accounts like that of Acts 16:25–34 which describe the conversion of Paul's jailer "and his entire household." This social unit, the household, the "natural" gathering of connected people, becomes the basis for the house churches that Paul founds.

The closest we have come to this household model has perhaps been the way in which geographic parishes functioned before the development of easy transportation. People knew those who lived near them, and interacted easily and frequently with them. Catholics who belonged to the same parish knew each other. There was significantly more interdependence. Their relational texture was not like that of the ancient household, of course; but the familiarity that a parishioner had with other people at Sunday Eucharist is not replicated in contemporary urban and suburban life.

The nearest thing to "household" in US culture is perhaps the extended family, which is often found in Hispanic/Latino communities. One can hope that this model will help teach us in the Catholic Church about our essential connectedness, and not disappear through cultural assimilation.

In the past year I visited small Christian communities in Eastern Africa. At a parish meeting of the pastoral leaders of twenty-four small Christian communities, I asked each one present to indicate, for my information, "how many people are in your community?" I know that people in the US would have counted the number of individuals and given an answer. But every one of the twenty-four community leaders said how many families are in the community, for family, not the individual person, is the basic social unit.

This desire for community life is increasingly vivid in the church as in wider culture. We both fear it and yearn for it.

"One Another": Mutuality as a Mark of Community

The Greek adverb *allelon* and a cognate *allelous* occur about 100 times in the New Testament. The Greek dictionary gives "mutually" and "reciprocally" as meanings. About forty of them occur in the Pauline and deutero-Pauline letters, nine of them in Acts, and twenty-four in the Johannine texts. In some instances the adverb simply notes things that people did together, e.g., "they said to one another 'Has no one brought bread...'" (Mk 8:16); or, "the shepherds said to one another 'Let us go to Bethlehem...'" (Lk 2:15); or, "the disciples said to one another 'Has someone brought food for him?'" (Jn 4:33).

Many of the passages in which this adverb appears are descriptive of the virtues and failures that characterize a Christian community. Mutuality is clearly a mark of the new people of God. In the fourth gospel Jesus tells the disciples that they must wash one another's feet (Jn 13:14). Especially telling in this gospel are the instructions of Jesus to the disciples (and, to the Johannine communities) to love one another (Jn 13:34,35; 15:12, 17). In the brief Johannine letters, community members are told that they participate in one another's lives (1 Jn 1:7), and are given the admonition to love one another (1 Jn 3:11; 3:23; 4:7; 4:11; 4:12; 2 Jn 5).

In the Pauline materials there is great clarity concerning the mutuality that should be found in the communities. Paul speaks of his longing to visit the Roman community in order that both he and they might be strengthened by a faith that is mutual between them (*allelois*) (Rom 1:12). There are many gifts in the community, but all of the holders of these gifts belong to the body of Christ, so the gifts belong to them mutually (*allelon*) (Rom 12:5). All are to love each other in their faith as siblings together (*allelous*) (Rom 12:10).

There is a statement in Romans 12:16 whose power depends upon the verb used, one which does not have an easy English translation. In Greek thought, with which Paul was familiar, there is a kind of knowledge we can have about the kind of world we should be making. If we know what should be done, we are implicated in the doing of it. We cannot know what is the right thing to do and not do it, and still be virtuous. Aristotle calls this knowledge and its implementation *phronesis* and *praxis*. Paul asks that all community members reach a mutual understanding about what needs to be done and mutually collaborate in the doing of it, *eis allelous phronountes*.

All Christian communities are called to a mutuality which exists because we belong to a single body. The good of one and the good of all are interdependent. Each of us recognizes how many decisions we make each day based upon our personal routines: where I will be at noon, this afternoon, next week, next summer, next year. All those are about my future. Mutuality exists when the future of others weighs into my decision-making.

For the last fourteen years I have lived in a large, old New Orleans house, what people here call "a double." On one side is a small community of professed religious Marianist men. On the other side is a lay Marianist family. The wife/mother is a counselor in a Catholic girls high school; the husband/father a campus minister in a Catholic co-ed high school. The children are thirteen, five, and three years old. I am often moved by how often one of the adults, or both, and sometimes the children, give up their own preferences and needs, for the sake of one of the other's preferences or needs. I am sure that sometimes it is a painful surrender. But it happens and not frequently. That is a great lesson for our side of the house. Making a decision for one's own future that incorporates the future of another is not the rule in American life, nor is making personal decisions for the common good.

In the latter part of this chapter I want to discuss the practice of mutuality in immediate community living. In the chapter on mission, I will discuss mutuality in the service of any community's deep story, and in putting that deep story to work in addressing critical human needs. We are called to be *allelon* to the core.

Community and Church

> It has pleased God to make us holy and save us not merely as individuals without any mutual bonds, but by making us into a single people, a people which acknowledges God in truth and serves God in holiness. (*Lumen Gentium*, 9)

When the Second Vatican Council began its dogmatic constitution on the Church with a presentation of Church as the people of God, a major shift in the Catholic thinking was occurring. The shift continued when the apostolic responsibility for the life of the Church was said to be grounded in baptism rather than ordination or religious profession. Yet these latter two are critically important further specifications of how God calls us to assume our baptismal apostolic responsibility.

There has been corresponding shift from seeing baptism as a redress of a primary emphasis on the consequences of original sin to seeing it as initiation into a community, into the people of God. The two views are, of course, closely related, for the community called Church mediates the grace that redeems us from "original sin."

The Rite of Christian Initiation for Adults is a restoration of the socialization process of the early church for initiating new members into the community called church. It is common practice for an RCIA team to guide a catechumen through the stages of catechumenate, through baptism, and through a brief period of mystagogy, so that the new member of the community can be apprenticed to real community. And that community would be involved in important ways in the formation process. The new Church member, then, will be situated in the life of a functioning community.

Small Christian communities, also called base communities, are a growing ecclesiastical phenomenon. In the US Catholic Church there

are between 40-50,000 of them, very loosely organized and/or coordinated. But they are there, searching for community and a spiritual life.
The recovery of community is afoot. We need our "peopleness" back.

Pope John Paul II has called continental synods to address the
issues and challenges that face Catholicism today. In the exhortation
response to the synods, there is clear support and encouragement for
the formation of small Christian communities. The following statements are from the papal exhortations, *Ecclesia in Africa*, paragraph 89
(*Origins*, Oct 5, 1995), *Ecclesia in Asia*, paragraph 25 (*Origins*, Nov. 18,
1999), and *Ecclesia in America*, paragraph 41 (*Origins*, Feb. 4, 1999).

> The church as family cannot reach her full potential as church unless
> she is divided into communities small enough to foster close human
> relationships. It seems entirely timely to form ecclesial communities
> and groups of a size that allows for true human relationships.
>
> Ecclesial communion implies...a 'participatory' church....Every
> member's unique charism needs to be acknowledged, developed,
> and effectively utilized...In this context...the Synod fathers under-
> lined the value of basic communities as an effective way of promot-
> ing communion and participation....
>
> One way of renewing parishes, especially urgent for parishes in large
> cities, might be to consider the parish as a community of communities
> and movements. They should be places engaged in evangelizing them-
> selves so that they can subsequently bring the good news to others.
> They should be communities that pray and listen to God's word,
> encourage the members to take responsibility, learn to live an ecclesial
> life, and reflect on different problems in the light of the gospel.
>
> These small groups help the faithful live as believing, praying, and
> loving communities like the early Christians. In such a human con-
> text it will be easier to hear the word of God, to reflect on the range
> of human problems in the light of this word, and gradually to make
> responsible decisions inspired by the all-embracing love of Christ.
> They are a solid starting point for the building of a new society, the
> expression of a civilization of love.

In an age increasingly described as postmodern, the need to reinvent community for our times is urgent. Community, though never

easy to achieve, is most possible when there is substantial agreement about basic concerns.

Given the kind of pluralism that historical consciousness affirms is not always transcendable, how do people form community? Something new is needed. People who differ on basic concerns can at least agree on guidelines that can shape their togetherness and discourse. First, each will always speak with the purpose of giving the other the best chance of understanding what the speaker believes and why. If the speaking has as its objective to convince the other, the dialogue will go no further. Second, each will listen with the intention of understanding the speaker on the speaker's own terms. Third, both agree ahead of time not to leave the conversation. Fourth, all participants will focus on the implications for lived experience that proceed from any and all positions.

One presupposition here is that whenever I am exposed to the experience of genuine otherness, I will not come away the same as before. I may not agree, but my world of understanding is larger, and I will almost certainly have come to understand my own position better. In the face of pluralism, there is a soft relativism that says "Well, that's your opinion, and I have mine." But there is a tougher road that lays even heavier weight upon the importance of truth claims, often best clarified through any position's consequences in the world. So what? This kind of community is sometimes referred to as dialogic community, and there is plenty of room for it in religious life and in the church generally.

The rather sudden emergence of base communities on every continent, adapted in each place to local needs and local forms of community living underscore the need for models of community. We are experimenting with base communities. There is some institutional support, although this is very recent, and various models are being tried. Religious communities, small Christian communities, and experiments in dialogic community have every reason in the world to form close alliances. They have so much to teach and learn from one another (*allelon*).

Community Life and US Culture

After visiting the Unites States in the 1830s, Alexis de Tocqueville wrote *Democracy in America*, in which he described individualism as a notable characteristic of our culture:

> Individualism is a calm and considered feeling which disposes each citizen to isolate himself from the mass of his fellows and withdraw into a circle of family and friends; with this little society formed to his taste, he gladly leaves the greater society to look after itself. (de Tocqueville, 1969, 506)

This judgment is corroborated by Ralph Waldo Emerson in his essay on "Self Reliance":

> Then, again, do not tell me, as a good man did today, of my obligation to put all poor men in good situations. Are they my poor? I tell thee, thou foolish philanthropist, that I grudge the dollar, the dime, the cent, that I give to such men as do not belong to me and to whom I do not belong. (Emerson, 1983, 70)

This motif appears as well in popular media. In the November, 1996, issue of *Bon Appetit* magazine, there is a full-page ad sponsored by the Independent Sector Ad Council. which shows a large paper cup, presumably filled with coffee, with the following words printed on the side of the cup:

> In America you are not required to offer food to the hungry or shelter to the homeless. There is no ordinance forcing you to visit the lonely, or comfort the infirm. Nowhere in the Constitution does it say that you have to provide clothing for the poor. In fact, one of the nicest things about living here in America is that you really don't have to do anything for anybody.

The ad is run in praise of the eighty million people who volunteered time and money during the previous year even though there was no civic obligation to do so. The intention of the ad is praiseworthy, but the cultural presupposition that underlies it is most certainly not biblical: we are not our brother's and sister's keepers. Or, to put it philosophically, connections between human beings, are external and accidental, not internal and constitutive. Caring is optional. That is not a good narrative structure.

Since the 1950s there have been numerous sociological appraisals of US culture addressing this individualism and its consequences: *The Lonely Crowd: A Study of the Changing American Character* (David Riesman, et al), *The Fall of Public Man* (Richard Sennett), *The Pursuit of Loneliness: American Culture at the Breaking Point* (Philip Slater), *Habits of the Heart: Individualism and Commitment in American Life* (Robert Bellah, et al), and *Loose Connections: Joining together in America's Fragmented Communities* (Robert Wuthnow). The human disconnect, reflecting perhaps a version of what freedom is held to mean, leaves people lonely at a cultural level, needing the very community to which we are fearful of committing. But community is not possible without commitment, and individualism makes that kind of commitment difficult, as Bellah and his colleagues detail so clearly in *Habits of the Heart.*

In his 1994 book, *Sharing the Journey: Support Groups and America's New Quest for Community*, Robert Wuthnow finds that four of every ten Americans now belong to some kind of small group, most of which are support groups or common interest groups. Wuthnow believes in the efficacy of these groups to instigate changes in American society (Wuthnow, 1995, 3). He feels that they are generating a better understanding of community and are actually redefining spirituality. He also says that these groups (the religious ones) are changing how God is understood. There is less emphasis upon external authority and more on an internal presence (ibid.).

While finding God within our experience is certainly a positive, the anger of God at an unjust world carries authority. A religious community's strong dialectic between need and prophetic Word (whether of Jesus or Isaiah or Amos) needs to condition small Christian communities. Wuthnow warns that a support-group culture for a small community runs the risk of domesticating God by having God take on the character of a support group member:

> Indeed, relational language prevails. People feel closer to God, experience God as a parent or friend, feel loved, and believe that a kind of mutual understanding has emerged between themselves and this divine companion....Yet there is also a danger if God becomes a being with the same characteristics as those experienced in one's

support group. The danger is that God becomes an instrument to make ourselves feel better.

But for some people, spirituality is domesticated at the same time that it is reinforced....Sacred ceases to be the *mysterium tremendum* that commands awe and reverence and becomes a house pet that does our bidding. God becomes a source of advice and comfort and the proof of God's existence becomes the group. Because the reality of the sacred depends on God's relevance to our lives, God becomes easier to understand and God's actions become smaller, modifying our attitudes and calming our anxieties, rather than moving mountains. But a domesticated view of the sacred has always been worrisome to the saints and sages who have struggles most deeply with its meaning and implication. (Wuthnow, 1995, 230-231, 255)

What gives religious community its best chance to encounter God without domesticating God is perhaps the conversation between faith and culture, with social analysis, and an impulse from the deep story to respond to critical needs, and, above all, concrete immersion in the world and "the joys and hopes, the griefs and anxieties of the people of this age, especially those who are poor or in any way afflicted..." (*Gaudium et Spes*, 1).

Any community that takes mutuality seriously runs the risk of becoming primarily a support group. The sensitivity groups of the 60s and 70s taught members of religious communities skills they could use in community. The appropriate sharing of deep feeling, for example, belongs to genuine mutuality. What insures a healthy perspective for religious communities, and for small Christian communities more generally, is the balance between the dynamics of being gathered and being sent, communally and individually.

A real Christian community is always both gathered and sent. The sending is a natural response to the dialogue of the gathered between our faith's deep story and the concrete exigencies of our world. It the duty of the prophetic voice to ask over and over and over, "So what?" To a text from Scripture, "So what?" To a social analysis, "So what?" To a new reading of the deep story, "So what?' We do not have to live in communities of religious life long to know how easy it is to domesticate God, and to domesticate as well our foundresses and founders.

The title of Robert Wuthnow's 1998 book tells a story all by itself: *Loose Connection: Joining Together in America's Fragmented Communities.* "Our lives," he writes, "are molded by social conditions that make looser connections seem more appropriate" (Wuthnow, 1998, 58). He notes, for example, that more than a third of those in their twenties change their residences every year. In 1950 the divorce rate was one in four marriages; currently the divorce rate is one in every two marriages. This change creates a climate that lowers people's expectations about marriage. If one out of ten marriages ends in divorce, divorce remains the exception. But when the record is one of out of two, cultural support for enduring marriages is greatly lessened.

Robert Bellah gave a talk recently at St. Mary's University in San Antonio, titled "Building Community in a Society of Loose Connections and Porous Institutions." He began with the reminder that "community is not some frill, some third thing that we take or leave, but is the fundamental truth of our condition...Without social interaction, without language, the biological individual will never fully develop into a human person; it is our very personhood and our respect for it, that we owe to society, to community" (Bellah, 2000, 3).

Today one finds many communities that are voluntary or disposable. People voluntarily enter them, but there is no obligation to remain. This is sometimes hailed as a right combination for Americans in that it invites grouping but respects the freedom of the individual to stay or not stay. Bellah, however, is convinced that disposable communities are antithetical to democratic freedom. As a model for grouping, such a cultural ideal is clearly hostile to family life, and certainly to Christian community.

In her book *The Human Condition*, Hannah Arendt names two features of reality that we must address. The first is that of "irreversibility." What has happened has happened and cannot be rewritten, Past is past. If the past has been a damaging past, only forgiveness can redeem it and let us move on. Forgiveness does not mean approval. Nor does it mean that we have not learned permanent lessons. Rather, it means that we choose to live forward. Christian life lives forward.

No social group is without its dark side which forgiveness addresses. Forgiveness is not naïve. It never absolves us from dealing with the consequences of our actions. But it lets us get on with it, keeping the social group intact.

The other feature of the human condition which Arendt names is unpredictability, the chaotic uncertainty of the future. She says that Abraham's experience with covenant had no other reason "than to try out the power of mutual promise in the wilderness of the word" (Arendt, 1958, 243-244). When we know that we can rely on promises made, the future loses some of its unpredictability. Mutual promising redeems the unpredictability of the human condition. Disposable communities cannot do that.

Looking back, it would seem that predictability was one of the hallmarks of American middle-class life. Parents could generally presume that their children would be better educated than themselves, and would be better off financially. Parents themselves were comfortable that their own jobs were not at risk, and they felt relatively secure. In 1950 the income from a forty-hour work week could support a middle-class lifestyle. Most of this is not true today. It takes two incomes to support a middle-class lifestyle today, both because the dollar buys less and because we have increased our expectations of what constitutes middle-class lifestyle: house size, number of automobiles, and private schools. Television and computers use up a lot of what might have been family time. The demands of work and school make shared meals a rare luxury. All of these threaten family cohesiveness.

There is a widening perception that not all is well with community life. Three-fourths of the public say that the breakdown of communities is indeed a serious national issue; and eighty-two percent say that people do not seem to care for each other as much as they once did (Wuthnow, 1998, 68). From 1970 to the mid-1990s the number of Americans living alone increased from 10.9 million to 23.6 million, which means that about one-fourth of households are single persons (Wuthnow, 1998, 74). This alone is symptomatic that something is amiss with community in our culture.

The "Virtuosi" and the "So what?" Question

The people who perceive the world with reasonable accuracy and then ask, "So what?" are very important, if often unnerving, to any social group. People who fit the category of "virtuosi" are often like that.

One of the sociological categories that Patricia Wittberg invokes to interpret religious life is that of Max Weber's "virtuosi." Despite the "aristocratic" connotation of the word. Wittberg says that the notion is helpful in recognizing that there are people in every organization or society who want the best that can be got, and have the resources and will to get it. "[I]t is the virtuoso who is driven by an interior hunger to devote his or her entire life to artistic, athletic, intellectual, or religious pursuits....The virtuosi of a society are those who are the most driven to find a solution to the increasingly insistent questions of their age" (Wittberg, 1996, 19, 62).

It used to be that religious life was mythologized as the life of perfection, and many virtuosi felt called to religious life for that very reason. Vatican II affirmed that all people are called to the same perfection. But marriage is no less a call to perfection as is the single life outside of religious life or priesthood. That demythologization of religious life is surely one of many factors that account for the sudden and steep decline in membership.

My sense of today's Catholic virtuosi is that they are found in three places. Some few continue to enter religious life or priesthood. Some become active in small Christian communities. And many are entering the ranks of lay ministry. There are, for example, more than twice as many lay people in graduate ministry programs as there are seminarians in four-year graduate programs. Not all who take up these options are virtuosi, but I regard these as the principal options for those who are deeply committed and gifted.

Wittberg says that religious communities must still appeal to Catholicism's virtuosi, and that "their success will depend upon whether or not they can uncover the 'sharpest anguish' of the twenty-first century and on how effectively they can formulate a spiritual answer to it" (Wittberg, 1995, 62). In her view "the most keenly felt cultural strain in our post-modern, Western society is not education, health care, or even the presence of some needy groups—as pressing as those other issues may be. Rather, it is a desire for community and spiritual depth" (Wittberg, 1995, 82-83).

Mercy and Justice in the Public Life
of Religious Communities

I am disinclined to name any one "anguish" as unquestionably the sharpest of all. But I believe that any list of them vis-à-vis US culture will have to place individualism vs. community very high on the list. Precisely because active, apostolic religious communities are communities, we are specially positioned to offer redemptive know-how to society at large.

Assigning a high priority to community does not mean that we should ignore other issues. I want to be very clear about that because concentrating on building and strengthening community in a first world nation might seem naive when compared to global issues such as poverty, war, nuclear proliferation, global warming, and so forth. But if active apostolic religious communities are to help address these issues, they must be first be solid, functional, interdependent, transforming communities. Therefore, I will continue to address community in terms of US culture, because I see it as a central issue in a nation that exports its culture across the globe.

Works of mercy address immediate human needs that must receive attention right now. Works of justice address dysfunctional systems that are responsible for injustice. Those of us in active apostolic religious communities recognize the satisfaction that we experience when we help meet immediate need. Because we care, that hands-on immediacy is rewarding. But if most of our efforts were directed to meeting immediate needs, we might find that we were only inadvertently strengthening the dysfunctional systems that produce those needs.

Over a number of years now I have observed an almost middle-class embarrassment at addressing social justice issues. Since Vatican II I have been on the faculty of four Catholic universities. When our institutes for pastoral theology offer workshops and lectures on social justice, the turnout is predictably small. But workshops and lectures on spirituality draw a large attendance.

It is easy for those of us who are middle-class folks to feel guilty for being middle class. I have no doubt that YHWH would prefer that every human being alive have access to the necessities, not merely for survival, but for a decent life. The resolution has more to do with such things as tax structures and minimum wage than for middle-class people to stop being middle class. If it takes $20,000 for a family of four to squeak through (and barely at that), the minimum wage would have to be ten dollars an hour for a full-time worker. Imagine the mobilization of public opinion that would be required for a change like that. My reading of the reign of God is that no one can have more than enough until everyone has enough, and that is a matter that rests primarily on social structures.

My experience in community is that we are at our best when some members are passionately committed to responding to immediate and critical human need, and others are responding to the transformation of critical social structures. These are two different kinds of experience and two different kinds of expertise, and together they stand a good chance of generating the passion, the wisdom, and the practical skills that are needed. It is a blessed community that has them both in dialogue, in prayer, and in mutual caring.

One of the obvious differences between base communities in Latin America and the United States is that a majority of those in Latin America are very poor, while small Christian communities in the United States tend to be better educated and slightly more affluent than the general Catholic population. While that is clearly a difference, there is an important similarity. In Latin America the organization of the large numbers of poor has built a power base for social change. In the United States, a conscientious middle class is an important power base for change. It is largely middle-class folks who built the civil rights movement, the peace movement, and participated effectively in the lettuce boycotts that empowered the Farm Worker Movement.

Most American religious come from middle-class families. It is a culture we understand. We are in it. It is in us. It is fruitful "missionary territory" once we understand its potential for instigating social change. Wittberg writes that

> To write off middle-class Euro-American culture as unable to produce a form of religious life that will address its own strains and discontinuities—as previous models had addressed the strains of their respective centuries—is to defect from our responsibility as religious to take part in the formation of one of the most influential "center" cultures of the world. (Wittberg, 1995, 78, her emphasis in the original)

A morally sensitive American middle class is a power base for social transformation. As religious communities become empowered by mutual nurturing between those in direct contact with critical human need and those with expertise to effect institutional change, they can attract virtuosi. A viable and strong deep story can be seen at work responding to human need and human longing. And I hope it is obvious that Word and Eucharist, as centerpieces for community prayer, are both what grounds a community and what makes flight possible, the beating of great wings:

If I don't manage to fly,
      someone else will.
The Spirit only wants
      that there be flying.
As for who happens to do it
      in that the Spirit
      has only a passing interest.

                              —Rainer Maria Rilke

Why not us?

Three Reflections on Community

In the concluding paragraphs of this chapter on community I want to address three questions. First, what are some implications of mutuality in single sex, celibate communities for the recovery of mutuality anywhere in Christian community? Second, how can we make our

deep story meaningful in contemporary culture? For this last reflection, I will have recourse to some insight in the process-relational
thought of Alfred North Whitehead. And finally, why is communal
living so crucial?

Mutuality in Celibate Communities

Religious life developed long before recent theories of developmental
psychology. Among the many theorists, I value the work of Erik
Erikson because of his interest in the stages of healthy development
rather than the pathologies. After adolescence, the stage of growing
into adulthood involves successfully addressing intimacy needs and
learning the skills of human mutuality. Most religious communities
recognize the many strictures against intimacy among their members.
Many of these structures are understandable and insightful.

Human attachments that restrict upon our availability to mission
are not healthy. Human attachments that can find their fulfillment
only genitally are clearly not healthy. While religious history pre-
serves wisdom in such matters as reserve and abstention, it has much
less wisdom to offer to the healthy function of intimacy and mutuality in celibate communities. We are trying very hard to create some
new wisdom. An adult person "should act in such a way that [s]he
actualizes both in him[her]self and in the other such forces as are
ready for a heightened mutuality" (Erikson, 1960, 413).

A married relationship and sexual intimacy are the usual contexts
for negotiating intimacy needs and learning the practice of mutuality.
Negotiating these adulthood challenges is not easy in celibate communities, and there is precious little historical experience to guide us.

The stage that normally follows a successful handling of intimacy
needs is that which Erikson calls generativity. In families where children are older and life is more settled, parents often feel heightened
concern for what kind of a world they want to help build for their
children. "Generativity is the creation of a new generation and as
such involves a desire to guide and to teach as well as to produce"
(Wright, 1982, 95).

Because it is not easy for celibate religious to negotiate intimacy
needs appropriately, largely because historical models for doing so are

not at our disposal, it is a temptation to jump into productive work. Productivity is easily valued and rewarded in both religious and civil culture. Wright cites Erikson's discussion of a Dr. Borg who "lost in love and withdrew (the polar vice of love) to become proficient in his profession. His longing for that lost love becomes an unresolved crisis ..." (Wright, 1982, 92). A comparable experience in religious life might be escape from facing up to valid intimacy needs by what can be a polar vice in young adults, being "damned good" in one's work and profession. To move prematurely into what looks like generativity, but without having developed adequately first in negotiating intimacy needs, is an almost sure route to burn-out by age fifty.

I don't want to oversimplify Erikson. Identity, intimacy, and generativity are not simply successive stages of development. We do not leave one stage once and for all. One never settles identity issues with utter finality, nor intimacy issues, nor those of generativity. Yet there are genuine developmental stages when one set of issues is clearly center stage and is more absorbing than the others.

It is difficult to be more specific than to speak of "appropriate" intimacy and "appropriate" expressions of mutuality. Appropriate disclosures between spouses is not the same as disclosures between members of a religious community. The deep stories of various religious communities will affect the nature of appropriateness. The age of community members will make a difference, as will the mix of ages. How long the people in a community have known each other matters. Certainty about confidentiality is another huge factor—in a word, trust. Trust is earned; it is not guaranteed by community membership.

If I could name one gift that needs to be present in a community to most facilitate healthy mutuality it would be competency in conflict resolution, or at least conflict management. There is no possibility that honest community, like honest friendship, can avoid conflict. The more diversity there is in a community, the more energy and interest are likely to abound, provided that inevitable conflict is addressed head on. Conflict is not a negative. It is an invitation to clarification, supportive tolerance, and deeper community.

In their book *Community of Faith*, Evelyn and James Whitehead offer a paradigm that is helpful for locating mutuality is a religious commu- nity. A primary group is a group whose principal reasons for being together are the relationships that bind them. Families and groups of friends are examples. A secondary group is a group whose primary rea- sons for being together have to do with some work or business or pro- ject. People who work in the same office, who belong to the same parish team, who are on the same soccer team are secondary groups.

The Whiteheads say that Christian communities are hybrid groups. They have some characteristics of a primary group, for Christians are sisters and brothers in Christ, bonded with each other through bap- tism (as well as through their shared humanity). They care about each other. Mutuality is a highly appropriate, even necessary, concern for members of a primary group. Paul's letters abound with advice about mutuality between community members.

But followers of Jesus are also always people in permanent mission, collaborating with God to realize God's intentions for human history. They have a project together, which gives them the characteristics of a secondary group. They have to learn how to collaborate together for reasons that transcend their comfort with each other—"there is some- thing larger than our relationship that drives us."

The fact that a community is a secondary group in mission pro- vides a context for mutuality in its primary group configuration. Conflict should never be avoided, but its perceived importance can be diminished by the great common tasks of mission. People on the same work force do not have intimacy as an immediate concern. Obviously, good relations improve their ability to do their tasks well. The mutuality that a religious community in its primary group con- figuration brings to mission is full of grace for mission.

Briefly, that fact that communities of active apostolic religious com- munities are both primary and secondary groups helps define what is appropriate intimacy and mutuality. If there is inadequate attention to mission, the primary group dynamics can assume a centrality that is not appropriate. If there is inadequate attention to the community as primary, mission will be deprived of some relational power that befits apostolic teams.

Survival and Intensity

In the years following closely upon to Vatican II, I used a paradigm from Alfred North Whitehead's philosophy to speak about survival and intensity in the life of the church (Lee, 1974, 199-202). I will here apply that paradigm to active, apostolic religious communities.

The language of survival and intensity will shift to surviving and thriving, mostly because in popular usage "intensity" is often a pejorative term. But to live with some degree of intensity entails a high degree of responsiveness to one's environment. It requires a complex structure to adapt well and quickly to changes in environment. The requirements for survival and intensity are at odds with each other.

In good times and bad, every religious order desires to survive. In any organism the desire to live is strong. We religious usually believe that we have a contribution to make to God's reign; we want to do it, and to keep on doing it. The desire to survive is a strong and good natural impulse, as long as we also accept the finitude of both personal lives and institutions, and can recognize when our time has come. Survival remains an intense drive.

One condition that favors survival is having a very simple, uncomplicated structure with few moving parts. There is less than can go wrong. The fewer the requirements, the easier the going. A simple structure is far easier to maintain. Further, any society, like any organism, that is not tightly connected with and dependent upon an external environment can more easily survive changes in that environment.

Thriving is related to the dynamics that give a deep story its best chance of reinventing charism. As the Nygren/Ukeritis study indicates, a community's responsiveness to critical, unmet human needs generates the relevance that improves the chances of survival. But the kind of detailed interaction between the social environment and the mix of action and structures needed to respond quickly and effectively are the opposite of the requirements for survival. These latter are very complex.

The challenge for any religious congregation is to combine surviving and thriving. At the highest level of organization, a congregation should understand itself and articulate itself in very accurate but very large sweeps, capable of hugely diverse modes of implementation. At that level, the challenge to do one's best elicits a sense of the deep story, which, of course, can never be fully told. Every edition of the Constitution or Rule of Life is but one more particular story striving to say something true and significant about the deep story.

We are all familiar with efforts to name defining characteristics for our time. In my congregation, we have fashioned documents for US communities about Marianist characteristics of secondary education, university education, and parishes. At the international level we have named characteristics of Marianist formation. I think every congregation has comparable documents. These are our attempts to express the deep story in its purest articulation to guarantee vigor and responsiveness at the local level and survival at the universal level.

Satisfaction at the local level nourishes the will to survive. We expect to derive some satisfaction from the fact that we have been able to meet some real need. I do not take satisfaction to mean some kind of "mere" enjoyment, but the satisfaction we experience when the right thing is done well, precisely requiring our profound involvement in the details of life. This involves a lot of interaction with events and people around us. That involved interaction is what Whitehead calls intensity. In this context, thriving is all tied up with a successful handling of many "moving parts." It frequently requires very sophisticated and particular structures to enable a group to be responsive to their immediate environment. There should, therefore, be maximum freedom for the adaptation of that centrality at the level of each local community, with structures of accountability to the larger community, including assessments.

The best mix will be marked by the absolute centrality of Eucharist and Word, framed by a defining dialectic between the world and the deep story.

Living Together

Active, apostolic religious congregations are communities-in–permanent-mission. The deep story, of course, lives in each member. If the church itself has virtuosi, many of whom become members of religious communities, each congregation as well has virtuosi, members who are especially committed, energetic, and articulating personal expressions of the deep story. Such people are critical to any community's energy and health.

But the story is a community story, and its primary embodiment is to be found in social systems as large as the entire congregation and its activities, and in the smallest local community and its activities.

I have lived most of my religious life in a Marianist community, but I have also lived as a lone Marianist in a city without a Marianist community. People knew that I was a Marianist, but no one experienced the Marianist deep story in me alone, for it is a corporate deep story and requires a corporate incarnation. I feel in retrospect that my presence was an incomplete Marianist presence. Certainly living together with other members of one's congregation is normative.

This is what the "Future of Religious Orders in the United States" had to say on the subject:

> Many religious have migrated to the periphery of their congregation, often living lives that reflect significant ministerial contributions but which have little to do with their congregations or religious life. For many such persons the call by the congregation to participate in its vocation or mission would be welcomed. For others, the dynamics of individualism and "inner authority" have come to dominate over any notion of vocation that entails either obedience or even discernment of the will of God in the context of a congregational commitment. (Nygren/Ukeritis, 1992, 271)

We are realistic enough to know that it is not possible in a congregation to involve the entire membership in an ideal form of communal life. One reason is that we have sometimes supported individuals working outside a community context, and this has created some history that cannot be reversed in a moment. Another reason is that there are always some members who are so disruptive that they are not healthy for community and community is not healthy for them. But pathologies should not alter the normative mode.

And finally...

To be a follower of Jesus whose project is the reign of God is to belong to a gathering of people which the Greek language calls *ekklesia*, and which we have come to call church as well as community (the two are more interchangeable than popular usage suggests). Religious communities are uniquely suited for a sacramental role both within the church and within US culture. For our sacramentality to be effective, we must increasingly attend to how our life together and its dynamics are exposed to church and culture, and be open to different forms of participation by those who are not members of our congregations.

While I have not addressed the growing movement of lay associate communities in this book, that phenomenon may be one of the most graced developments in religious life, where the deep story undergoes some remarkable new creativity through the mutual explorations of lay and religious. I believe that the issue is not just lay participation in "our" deep story, but our willingness to turn the religious deep story loose and encourage and support a fully lay appropriation of it. While we would remain in dialogue with this new development, we would surrender control over what the lay appropriation looks like. We would share proprietorship, which is the best guarantee for a shared stewardship.

At this writing, CARA and the National Association for Religious and Associates are preparing research on the phenomenon of associates in religious communities. We look forward to deepening our understanding of this new moment of grace.

FOR DISCUSSION

1. This is about your community's public life. "Corporate personality was" a Hebrew experience of collective identity. The New Testament says that the "kingdom of God" shaped the identity of Jesus and his disciples. How does your community's mission shape your collective identity and distinguish you from other communities?

2. This is about your community's inner life. How does mission shape the mutuality that functions among you? What is appropriate and inappropriate self-disclosure?

3. A safe prayer intention is "for the poor and suffering"; an unsafe prayer intention is "for the courage I need to address a dysfunctional relationship that subverts my ministry." What community members talk about when they have meals together is often a clue to their prayer intentions. Does that statement reflect your own experience?

4. Much has been written about the depth and tenacity of individualism in US culture. It cannot but leave its mark—both its achievements and its debilitations—on our religious lives. For better and for worse, how does individualism show up in your community's inner life? In your community's mission and ministry?

SEVEN

VOWS-IN-PERMANENT-MISSION

Introduction

I want to say again, as I said at the beginning, that I am not attempting a systematic treatment of religious life nor, in this chapter, a systematic treatment of religious vows. These are meditations about our religious vocation in the world. We are communities in permanent mission. My interest in the reflections that follow focuses on the contextualization of the vows in respect to mission.

Religious life springs from the imagination of the Church under the guidance of the Holy Spirit. It does not have a "nature." It has a defining history that has had many phases and will have many more, because there is more history to come. Although religious congregations practice celibacy, poverty and obedience, not all of them take the same three "vows," yet the basic obligations are the same.

The idea of leaving all and selling all to follow Jesus Christ is grounded in the New Testament as is becoming a eunuch for the sake of the reign of God. These are counsels, not requirements. They are undertaken for the work of Jesus Christ, his mission.

There is nothing in the New Testament which specifically supports a call for obedience as an evangelical counsel, although there are remarkable passages about how leadership and authority should function, and obedience should be understood in that concept. The presumption is that all social structures have leadership, and lawful leadership should be honored. Nor is there a scriptural call to put celibacy, poverty, and obedience together as a community format. But the Christian imagination went to work very early to create new life forms responsive to the Good News of Jesus Christ. Religious life is one of them and their incredibly rich variety has blessed church life.

There is, as Sandra Schneiders documents so clearly (Schneiders, 2000, 5-18), something clearly archetypal about religious life. The Essenes are a Jewish example. Long before the appearance of Christianity, monastic communities were a part of Buddhist life. Though very different in religious character, both Rome and Greece had vestal virgins. The religious charism of celibacy is rare in any general population; but it is a genuine charism, and it is profoundly efficacious when it occurs.

Religious life, as *Lumen Gentium* (#44) affirms, does not belong to the hierarchical structure of the church. Nor are religious communities part of the laity, for they have a separate canonical existence. I would guess that at the experiential level, active apostolic congregations have deep affinities for lay life, for even as celibate communities, they are profoundly rooted in the world.

Celibacy

Sexuality and the Impetus towards Relationality
There are the differences between women and men in the experience of celibacy, as reported in the Nygren/Ukeritis study of religious life (Nygren/Ukeritis, 1992, 266). Women are more likely than men to experience spiritual meaning in celibacy. I expect that men are more likely to embrace celibacy for its practical value in mission.

I believe that to make sense to our world today, a deliberate celibate commitment must embrace a strong affirmation of sexuality, and of the continuing positive and creative role of sexuality in the lives of people who have made a celibate commitment. What is positive and creative for the sexuality of celibates is, of course, not identical to what is positive and creative for those who are married.

There is no intrinsic value in abstaining from the conjugal love between a wife and a husband, nor from deliberately choosing not to procreate. Jephthah, about to go into battle with the Ammonites, made a vow to God:

> "If you deliver the Ammonites into my grasp, whatever first comes first out of the doors of my house to greet me when I return, that shall belong to YHWH, and I shall sacrifice it as a burnt offering."
>
> Jephthah crossed over into Ammonite territory to attack them, and YHWH delivered them over to him...
>
> When Jephthah returned to his house at Mizpah, his daughter came out to meet him She was dancing to the sound of tambourines. This was his only child; apart from her he had neither a son nor a daughter. When he saw her he tore his clothes and exclaimed, "Oh my daughter, what misery you have brought upon me....I have made a promise to YHWH that I cannot take back." She replied, "Father, you have made a promise to YHWH; deal with me however the promise requires...."
>
> She then said to her father, "Grant me this. Let me be free for two months. I shall go and wander in the mountains, and with my companions bewail my virginity." He replied, "Go." And he let her go for two months. (Judges 11, passim)

So she went away with her companions and bewailed her virginity in the mountains. When the two months were over, she went back to her father, and he treated her as the vow he made required of him. She had remained a virgin.

There are of course mythical elements interwoven with whatever actually transpired. But what is attested is the deep respect and honor for conjugal love. Virginity is not of itself a value. This is a very strong affirmation of sexual love, such that its absence is cause for grieving. But something as great as the needs of the reign of God can evoke this exceedingly generous offering to God, whence it becomes truly a holy sacrifice.

Andrew Greeley, in his book *Sexual Intimacy,* reminds married people that the choice of a marriage partner does not mean that they henceforth will not find other people sexually attractive and interesting. The fact that they choose not to act genitally on the attraction springs directly from another choice made in their marriage commitment.

I think it worth making a similar affirmation for celibates in religious life. Celibacy does not mean that henceforth we will not find other people sexually attractive and interesting. The fact that celibates choose not to act genitally on the attraction springs directly from their deliberate choice of celibacy. The "choice not to act" on sexual attraction in certain ways for both married and celibate men and women requires a life of discipline and practice. But some of the most important features of our sexuality and of sexual attraction do not thereby cease to function. Process theologian Henry Nelson Wieman writes:

> Sexuality breaks down the egoism which otherwise confines individuals and makes them profoundly responsive not only to one other person but to all persons and interests associated with the loved one. Human sexuality does not necessarily undergo all this, but it provides the biopsychological condition without which it could not happen. (Wieman, 1946, 238; non-inclusive language modified)

The reign of God could easily be substituted for the loved one in the above text, and the way that sexuality breaks down egoism and serves God would still apply. Sexuality provides for celibates as well the biopsychological condition that breaks down relational resistances (egoism).

Wieman continues that "the great disaster of human life is not the failure to attain the biological fulfillment of sex... [but] the failure to love under the impetus of sex to the height and depth that love can reach..." (Wieman, 1946, 238). In this text, sexuality means what Wieman calls "the coercive outreaches" (ibid.), the impulse towards relationality, nurtured and shaped by the rich complexities of womanhood and manhood. The coercive outreach to relationship is essential to the religious impetus towards conversion:

> A great love unrequited or otherwise fulfilled, provided that it does not produce bitterness and protective regression, will be effective in

opening the way for the work of creative transformation. Perhaps nothing is more effective. Religious commitment is no doubt necessary; but if it is to be truly effective in delivering the individual [or community] over into the power of creative transformation, it must build on that profound and revolutionary responsiveness derived from sexuality. (ibid.)

The Hebrew deep story has a strong sense of the power of human affectivity in the world's creative transformation, consistent with Wieman's words above. Hebrew anthropology puts the seat of personhood in the heart rather than the mind. Creative transformation is not for passionless people. We ask the Spirit to fill the hearts of the faithful and to enkindle in them the fire of love, and that is what remakes the face of the earth. This way of praying is deeply rooted in our tradition.

A Theological Discursus

Eros includes all of the impulses related to genital sexuality, but is far more encompassing. Eros includes the full range of experiences that invite responses of satisfaction and pleasure: children's laughter, cold water on a hot day; hot chocolate on a cold day; cloud formations in a bright sky; colors splendidly coordinated in Guatemalan fabric; the first ray of morning light; the first morsel of food that breaks the night time fast; or just things turning out right. The multiple blessings each day that the rabbinic tradition encourages are expressions of thanksgiving to God, and as such they promote enjoyment of all the gifts of God that occasion the blessings. And the world is full of them. Enjoyment of God's extravagant goodness is, in fact, an essential basis for the virtue of gratitude.

When God's perfection is looked at from the perspective of Greek thought, he is seen as complete, entirely and eternally happy and fulfilled. There is no new satisfaction that can modify the experience of God. While we may speak "anthropologically" about pleasing God, we "know" that God is already happy. There is no eros in God, only agape, a love that only gives but does not receive benefit and pleasure in a love returned. If there is no eros in God's life, then human eros is unable to sacramentalize of God's love because it has no resemblance to God's life. Nevertheless, the mystics often use the image of eros to speak of the experience of God. And Scripture calls the church the bride of Christ.

When God's perfection is viewed from the perspective of Hebrew thought about perfect love, God can be described as grieving or elated by all that we do. God yearns for us to live according to his intentions. In this framework, we can speak "anthropologically" about the eros of God, for new and genuine pleasure is a real possibility. And in this case, human eros can teach us about God and our relationship with God.

The sexual imagery for God's relationship with Israel, from God's mouth in Ezekiel 16, is very vivid. YHWH speaks:

> On the very day of your birth, there was no one there to cut your navel cord, no one there to wash you clean in water, no one to rub salt in, and no one to wrap you in swaddling clothes. No one even looked at you with enough pity to be moved out of sympathy to attend to you. On the day you were born, you lay there exposed in open fields in your own dirt.
>
> But as I passed, I saw you there kicking on the ground in your own blood. I said to you, "Live!' And I made you grow just like the grass in the fields.
>
> You developed and you grew and you reached the age for marriage. Your breast grew firm. Your hair was long and lovely. But you were completely naked. And I saw you as I was passing by. Your time had come, the time for love. So I spread my own cloak over you and I covered your nakedness. I swore to you and made a covenant with you, and you became mine.
>
> I bathed you in water and washed the blood from you. I anointed you with oil. I gave you dresses with fine embroidery, beautiful leather shoes, headbands made of linen, and a cloak made of silk. I gave you abundant jewels, bracelets for your wrists and a necklace around your throat. I placed a lovely diadem on your head. You were loaded down with gold and silver. You wore linen, silk, and brocade.
>
> For food, you had the finest flour to be found, and honey, and oil. You grew more and more beautiful. You rose to become queen. Your

beauty was famous through all the nations, because I clothed you with my own splendor.

It is clear that YHWH found Israel beautiful and that YHWH was deeply moved and pleased by her beauty.

I return to Wieman's description of sexuality as a biopsychological base for coercive outreaching for relationship, and think that God is not merely neutral and available for relationship with us, but yearns for us. Abraham Heschel evens speaks of God's "search" for us. Francis Thompson catches the same theme when he speaks of God as the "Hound of Heaven."

There is no good English word for the French adjective *disponible*. It is often translated as "available." But that word is too neutral. *Disponible* is more like sitting on the edge of your chair, leaning forward out of readiness and eagerness to be met. The coercive outreaching towards relationality makes us *disponible*, which James Joyce captured splendidly in Molly Bloom's words: "...and then I asked him with my eyes to ask again yes and then he asked me would I yes... and I put my arms around him and drew him down to me so he could feel my breasts all perfume yes and my heart was going like mad and yes I said yes I will yes."

Christian faith posits a God who loves the world with such power and such will-to-relationship that in the power of sexual attraction there is something real about the character of God's love (Lee, 1976, 380). By sexual attraction I do not mean to name only the desire for genital union, but our deep, pervasive need for relationship with other men and women and, most of all, with God. The struggle for us is to say "Yes" even when on the surface there is no desire to say "Yes." Our "yes" is not only uttered to those whom we easily find interesting. There is no one who as a child of God, and therefore as a sister or brother to me, is not interesting as a family member, as one whom God loves. Paul uses "Yes" as a christological category, leaving no room for a "Yes" and a "No":

> Do you think that what I am up to is based on ordinary human promptings so that I can say "Yes, yes" at the same time as "No, no"? As surely as God can be trusted, I am not saying to you both a "Yes"

and a "No." The Jesus Christ, the Son of God whom Silvanus, Timothy and I proclaimed to you, was never a "Yes" and a "No." His nature is all "Yes." He is a "Yes" to all of the promises of God. (2 Cor 1:17-20)

Realistically, human imperfection means that, no matter what our striving, our relational Yes is never as unqualified as that of Jesus'. Paul wanted, in his own words, to be all things to all people, yet could not get along well enough with John Mark to be willing to travel with him.

That having been said, relational generosity should be characteristic of celibate life, drawing upon the resources of our womanhood and manhood. Our traditions have ample reminders of the practice and the prudence that celibate relationships ask of us, but they are neither binders nor blinders. If, as Erik Erikson holds, successfully negotiating intimacy is a necessary stage of healthy adult development, we know well enough in celibate life that emotional intimacy easily and naturally invites sexual intimacy. Married people in their intimate relationships with others than their spouses know this tension too. We do not run from intimacy. But we follow the practices that these delicate and fragile outreachings require of us.

Celibacy above all has to power to call celibates to a larger relational world, larger and deeper, not smaller and shallower. After years as dean of the divinity school at the University of Chicago and professor of philosophical theology at Berkeley's Graduate Theological Union, Bernard Loomer was asked to name what seemed to him most important in his life. His answer has much that could be integrated into a celibate spirituality. Loomer called it s-i-z-e:

By s-i-z-e I mean the stature of your soul, the range and depth of your love, your capacity for relationships.

I mean the volume of life you can take into your being and still maintain your integrity and individuality; the intensity and variety of outlook you can entertain in the unity of your being without feeling defensive or insecure.

I mean the strength of your spirit to encourage others to become freer in the development of their diversity and uniqueness.

I mean the power to sustain more complex and enriching tensions.

I mean the magnanimity of concern to provide conditions that enable others to increase in stature.

To me, this is the fundamental category, this is the essential principle. (Cargas/Lee, 1976, 70)

None of us can love with the size of God's love. Loomer's formulation recognizes that there are limits to what we can take in and keep our integrity. But who of us has not amazed him/herself by engaging in new experiences that would have undone us in an earlier time, because our understanding was too limited, or our tolerance too narrow.

And I want to add another dose of realism. While celibacy has the potential for opening hearts and spirits, it also can generate a lifestyle that is quite closed-in, selfish, and not very available (certainly not *disponible*). Further, celibacy sometimes yields to the temptation to "protect" it by avoiding relationships with any enduring commitment, without ever acknowledging responsibilities to and for other human beings. These are soul-shriveling habits of being, and we know that they happen.

Celibacy as Pragmatically Strategic

As I said at the beginning of both this book and this chapter, these reflections are selective. I have passed over treatments that others have done well, or that a long tradition has addressed effectively. One such is the spirituality of celibacy as a basis for a profound personal relationship with God.

The practical and strategic advantages of celibacy for communities in mission do not figure prominently in celibate spirituality, almost as if the "merely" practical advantages were less worthy reasons for such a radical choice.

It would be a mistake to underplay the nature of the sacrifice in choosing not to have a conjugal relationship with a committed partner, in choosing to forgo the procreation of children and participation in the kind of family life that Vatican II called "a school of deeper humanity" (*Gaudium et Spes*, #52). Since I began this book manuscript, I have been called from a city, a community, a ministry commitment, and a local mission (after fourteen years) to move to another city and accept a mission there that seems very appropriate to my experience. The deep pain felt at "being dislodged" and the genuine exhilaration of the new call do not cancel each other out.

Celibacy as a lifestyle is what makes our *disponsibilité* to mission work effective when there is new need to be met for the reign of God. We pick up and leave, and sometimes offer heartbreak as a gift to God whose heart understands.

Mission is certainly not the only context for praising celibacy. But for active, apostolic communities, mission is a validating, redeeming context for celibacy—a reason that connects us to God and God's work, a fully practical spirituality at the heart of things of the heart.

Poverty

Two thoughts undergird these reflections on poverty. First, we should so live that the goodness of the word and its resources sustain all people, enabling them to live a decent human life. A wretched, destitute life is terrible. There is nothing lovely or worth celebrating in poverty itself. A poster from the 1960s proclaimed in bold letters, "Poverty sucks!" And that about says it. But when it does happen, there is a lot to be learned from it.

As I wrote earlier, it is important never simply to find Christ in the poor, but to find Christ in our identification with everything in them that wants to escape poverty. Second, those who followed Jesus can be classified by lifestyle. There were the itinerants who left home and traveled with Jesus as he moved around in the Galilee and Judea (with occasional forays into non-Jewish surroundings). That was a style of life that meant leaving a lot behind, and living, it seems, from a common purse (which Judas kept). This lifestyle greatly facilitates being able to pick up and go wherever the work of the reign of God requires.

Paul was a consummate itinerant. And then there are those who can be called "residents." The best example from the gospels would be Martha, Mary, and their brother Lazarus, or Cleopas and his wife who lived in Emmaus. It is clear that Jesus could not have called everyone to the itinerant form of discipleship, which would be harmful to family life, to marriage and children, and surely to the economy of any society. Most who accepted Jesus became resident followers. When we read the gospels it is often helpful to sense whether Jesus is teaching the itinerant twelve, the resident followers, or everybody.

As a lifestyle, religious are not bound to either model. The Dominicans, an Order of Preachers, and the Jesuits, who were founded to go wherever the Church asks them to go, lean towards the itinerant form. Monasteries have a resident orientation, although they have also sponsored missionary work. Many active, apostolic religious communities have sponsored institutionalized forms of apostolic missions, such as hospitals, primary and secondary schools, universities, orphanages, and the like. These apostolates are usually supported by resident communities, although their members are often asked to move.

Perhaps most communities of apostolic religious are sociological hybrids of these two forms. The presence needed to support institutional commitments often requires stability of personnel, i.e., a resident apostolic form. Yet we remain ever on call to relocate when a new combination of needs, gifts, and experience is needed somewhere else, and we readily say "Yes, I'll go." The material resources needed to support life as "resident-itinerants" is a call that must be made according to circumstances and solid, ascetic judgment. Mission is what frames that ascetic judgment. Whether resident, itinerant, or "hybrid," following Jesus for the sake of God's reign in the world in the why of it all.

The demands of mercy and justice frame God's self-disclosure in the Hebrew Scriptures and in the message of Jesus (especially in the synoptic gospels) about the shape of human life when God makes his intentions known. For over a century now, the Catholic Church has articulated how God's intentions impinge upon social and economic structures. When I name the dialogue between the Word and the world, between faith and culture, which is characteristic of Christian existence, I include the church's social teaching in Word. I stress again that this is not a "how to" book but a rambling set of meditations on the topic of religious life. Most generalizations are best left to specific congregations and communities for implementation. I would only suggest that this social teaching should have a large place in both initial formation and in ongoing social analysis.

One of the constant questions about the church's social teaching is "so what?"—not meaning, "what are the implications," but meaning "how can we do something about it that makes a difference?" In the social arena, a single individual alone has little power. The Industrial Areas Foundation reminds people often that there are two major power bases for social transformation: organized people and organized money. There are multiple organizations already in place so that we are never starting from scratch. I highly recommend *Catholic Social Action in the United States: A Guide to Organizations and Resources*, assembled by David O'Brien. In a word, poverty is not just a vow we take for our own lifestyle, but a lifestyle that promises strategic focus for our stewardship of the world.

A Brief Concluding Fantasy

I will share a fantasy, from my current New Orleans perspective, about local mission. There are two situations that frame the fantasy. The first is that New Orleans is a relatively poor city. The education of children from poor families, especially black families, is grossly inadequate because of the public system of education. The second defining situation has to do with the middle class.

As I noted before, in 1950 a middle-class family could live on the income generated by a single full-time wage earner. It would not have been fancy living, but neither would it have been wretched. There was job security. My father was a bank teller, and never had any reason to believe his job wouldn't always be there. Middle-class parents rightly believed that their children would almost certainly get a better education and better paying jobs than they had. Today it requires weekly income from eighty to ninety hours of work to sustain a middle-class lifestyle, which has altered the structure of family life in very basic ways, for both parents must work. Nor is there generally any reliable job security, or the presumption that our children will be better off. If this had happened in five years instead of fifty, middle-class folks would be up in arms.

The same dynamics that have disempowered the middle class have maintained and often deepened poverty. Alliances between the poor and the middle class could become an extraordinary power base for social change. But everything in our consumer culture works against such alliances, with the result that the poor are further disempowered.

My fantasy is a religious congregation that supports three communities in the same local area. The congregation accepts sponsorship for a school in a very poor area and a school in a middle-class area. The latter school charges higher tuition, and those who matriculate there know that and support it. There is one administration and one faculty who service both schools. There is one parent/teacher association. Some selected extracurricular programs are offered in each school with participants from both schools. A religious community anchors the endeavor. This community lives simply.

Similarly, two parishes, one poor and the other middle class, are served by the same pastoral team, and share the collection (which is higher from the middle-class parish, and they all know that). There is one pastoral team and one pastoral council for both. Each parish commits to encouraging the vision articulated by Pope John Paul II in his exhortation, *Ecclesia in America*, after the synods of the Americas, that parishes become a community of communities. Here again, a religious community anchors the endeavor. If there is a broad-based community organization in the area, both schools and parishes belong.

A third community services the four institutions in two ways. This community promotes the formation of small Christian communities in all four institutions. Second, it brings expertise in social analysis and theological reflection to parish councils, pastoral teams, school administrations and school councils, which it especially encourages through the small Christian communities, doing this above all in the dialogue between the Word, the world, and the community's deep story. This community also lives simply.

What I am trying to do here is imagine mission which addresses poverty in a real local setting in a way that is supported by the poverty commitment of a religious congregation, and which addresses both immediate need and systemic issues. I do not know if the fantasy is even workable in the manner presented. What remains is the fact that "poverty sucks" and we who take a vow of poverty have to have something pertinent to say to our brothers and sisters who are poor but not by choice.

Obedience

"What kind of a world do we want to live in, and what do we want to leave for our children?" "What does a worthwhile life look like?" These are the most important and basic questions in human life. It does not take long for any perceptive person to realize that "what kind of a world do I want?" is going to have to turn into a we question because our needs, wants, and desires run headlong into competing needs, wants, and desires. And consequently we get nowhere without compromise.

Christians understand that we are implicated in God's intervention in the unfolding of history. We celebrate and maintain all that corresponds to God's eros for the world, and we join our passions to God's on behalf of all the social transformation of which we stand in need. "Common good" is a singularly Catholic way of saying that we are in it together, and that no one ever has a separate destiny.

Our word "obedience" has an interesting etymology. It originates from two Latin words, *ob* and *audire*. One of the meanings of *ob* is "before," or "right in front of," as in obvious. *Audire* means "to listen" or "to hear." Obedience means standing directly in front of someone or something, listening carefully and giving a wholehearted response to what is heard. "Authority and obedience are exercised in the service of the common good" (*Evangelica Testification*, # 25). We position ourselves to listen intently and act accordingly.

Critical listening and critical responding for the common good of the world, of the church and its needs, of our congregation, of individual communities, of individual community members comprise fundamental reason for obedience in any situation. Listening must be both up and down. Victor Turner speaks of the difference in perspective and experience between *societas*, the large organizational structure, and *communitas*, the small units within the larger structure (Turner, 1977, 94-166).

Those involved in the operations of *societas* perceive and understand things that are not apparent to those in *communitas*. Maintenance issues are often paramount in the *societas*: what is good, what works—these should be maintained. *Communitas*, on the other hand, is nearer the social organization's front line. People here often feel the pulse and hear the heartbeat of contemporary experience more immediately because they are closer to the action. These two vantage points must not be stereotyped, for many of us "in the ranks" understand a lot about organizational dynamics, and many of us in administration understand those in the front lines.

The common good is served well when these two experiences "obey" each other, however they are housed. "Community life is the privileged place in which to discern and accept God's will, and to walk together with one mind and heart. ...Each individual engages in a fruitful dialogue with others to discover the Father's will" (*Vita Consecrata*, #92).

Two Notes on Dialogue

First, because of my emphasis on dialogue, I want to state the obvious before continuing. There are so many things to do in any community or congregation that it would be paralyzing to expect that every practical decision would be made through dialogue. One of the many functions of designated leadership is to make many of those decisions, the ones that are most nearly "just practical." That is why we need women and men in those positions who have earned the community's trust. And, no matter what, there will regularly be someone who says, "Why wasn't I consulted?"

Second, the emphasis on dialogue in the life of the community and on shared decision making is sometimes written off as Americanism. Similarly, the desire for more participative structures in the church is also sometimes similarly dismissed, "for the church is not a democracy." It is worth remembering that these impulses towards participative structures were born in the Western world in the eighteenth and nineteenth centuries, and maybe as far back as the Magna Carta (1215).

Simon Schama entitled his bicentennial book on the French Revolution, *Citizens*. His thesis in this book is that a cultural paradigm shift was being enacted, marking the end of the feudal system in which most people were subjects with little or no say-so, no political power or freedom. There is a new and strong desire to be citizens rather than subjects—citizens who share in the resources of the nation and in the decisions that affect the citizenry. Because institutional church culture was so deeply feudal, and so tenacious, hostility towards the church was fierce. In response to this hostility, the church dug in its feudal heels when it might have welcomed some lay exercise of responsibility.

Would that collegiality and subsidiarity had arrived much earlier. Both have received papal and conciliar support, although implementation has lagged. Both of these notions are supportive of the practice of leadership and authority. So we will look briefly at each of them as further contextualizations for obedience.

Subsidiarity

Pius XI endorsed the principle of subsidiarity in his encyclical *Quadragesimo Anno* (1931):

> It is...a disturbance of right order for a larger and higher organization to arrogate to itself functions which can be performed efficiently by smaller and lower bodies. This is a fundamental principle of social philosophy, unshaken and unchangeable, and it retains its full truth today. Of its very nature the true aim of all social activity is to help individual members of the social body, but never to destroy or absorb them. (#79)

> Let those in power, therefore, be convinced that the more faithfully this principle of subsidiary function be followed...the more excellent will be both the authority and the efficiency of the social organization as a whole and the happier and more prosperous the condition of the state. (#80)

The closer decisions are made to the lives they affect, the more likely will they be informed by the conditions of those lives. One can and should make use of whatever insight and expertise is available. Making decisions close to "where the rubber hits the road" is no absolute guarantee of success but it improves the odds. And the major benefit is that by participating in decision making those whom decisions affect exercise a greater degree of ownership.

Pius XI calls it a moral disorder not to practice subsidiarity. For a thorough presentation on this topic I recommend John Kelley's recent book, *Freedom in the Church: A Documented History of the Principle of Subsidiary Function*. This is not just a church issue, it is a human issue about which the church's social voice is one of the very clearest. It is no secret, however, that subsidiarity has not become a hallmark of institutional church life. Witnessing to subsidiarity in the very heart of ecclesial life just might be one of the prophetic gifts of religious life.

Collegiality

Webster's Dictionary describes collegiality as power invested equally among colleagues. Acts 15, sometimes wrongly described as the First Council, describes the collegial way of addressing a serious problem in the first century. There is a collegiality operative among the great Councils of the church. In religious communities provincial and general chapters are examples of collegial leadership of authority.

In response to signals from Vatican II, Paul VI made some initial strong moves to develop collegiality among bishops. While collegiality is not the same thing as subsidiarity, what they have in common is the distribution of power in a social body so that people have a real voice in the life they share. The Council noted that collegiality functions "in the conciliar assemblies which made common judgments about more profound matters in decisions reflecting the views of many" (*Lumen Gentium*, #22).

The use of consensus dynamics in decision-making is one form of support for collegial processes. Voting on sensitive issues often divides a community. Consensus processes take longer, but often succeed in energizing an entire group. The question often is not, "is this the decision you prefer," but "is this decision one that you can genuinely support, even if it isn't your first choice, since committed shared action will be so much more effective? Can you still be whole-hearted?" This is the question: what best serves the whole community? The perfect is often the enemy of the good.

Obedience is about responsibility for the common good. It applies to members within a religious congregation, and it applies to how religious congregations are responsible for their particular mission vis-à-vis the reign of God. Mission is really the organizing principle for the function of authority.

Finally, the etymology of "authority" offers an interesting gloss on all of these. The Latin verb *augere* means to cause something to grow or to thrive, to bring increase, or even to come into existence in the first place. *Auctor*, a noun form from the verb *augere*, is someone who fosters growth, or brings something into existence. Thus, it sometimes means an author, one who tells the story, or even writes the story into existence. Obedience, then, is about authority, or better, about authorship: to whom do we give the power to co-write our story. In religious life, mission is the principal author[ity], our action conjoined with the action of God, which is nothing less than union with God—with our deep story woven into the plot.

For Discussion

1. According to Erik Erikson, negotiating intimacy needs is a universal stage of human development. Those who try to move into generativity (making their contribution to the world) without having negotiated intimacy needs often burn out very early. In your community patterns, what kinds of frameworks and supports are there for attending to normal human intimacy needs?

2. Given your community's deep story, what are some of the guidelines or expectations about lifestyle that are put forward? Some of them turn up in Rules of Life, some in legislation, and many are unspoken but operative (and those are the most difficult to discern, but have a lot of unspoken power).

3. If you agree with *Evangelica Testificatio* that "authority and obedience are for the common good," what issues would you like to see addressed in a leadership formation program?

EIGHT

DEEP STORY AS CULTURE IN CONGREGATIONALLY SPONSORED INSTITUTIONS

Introduction

I want to address the increasingly complex issue of congregational sponsorship of larger institutions (universities, large parishes, high schools and grade schools, hospitals, orphanages, etc.), because historically this has been one of the major modes of apostolic mission. Understanding the complexity of this form of apostolic mission provides an insight into any congregation's worldly spirituality. These are not new questions, but they have come up in my position as assistant chancellor in a university, with responsibility for nurturing the Catholic identity of that institution as well as the impact of my community's deep story, not just in a day to day way, but structurally as well.

I have distinguished early on, and throughout the book, between a deep story and a charism. I will focus here on deep story and its culture. If the congregational deep story permeates the institutional deep story so that it effectively identifies and addresses critical unmet human needs, then charism might indeed happen. Always there is the hope that the deep story can flourish as charism, not because *we* need it, but because the reign of God may so be served.

The sponsorship of large institutions as an apostolic commitment works well when there are large numbers of religious to staff the institutions. When this is not the case, we either develop alternative staffing patterns or look for options where large numbers of religious in the same place will not be required for effective missioning (I believe this will increasingly be the case in the foreseeable future).

The Association of Catholic Colleges and Universities (ACCU) conducted a study on the topic, suggesting that with the decline in numbers of members of sponsoring congregations, Catholic colleges and universities will go in one of three directions: and a few will simply become secular, public institutions in character; most will be generically Catholic; a few will find imaginative ways to maintain the effective presence of the sponsoring congregation. *Mutatis mutandis*; there are similarities within all of our sponsored institutional apostolates.

The study rightly noted that congregations were able to inform the cultures of institutions where they had sufficient numbers. Culture is informed first by social groups, and secondarily by the individuals who make up those social groups. Numbers are important because we cannot have social groups without members.

In this chapter I would like to propose an understanding of culture, applicable to both institutional cultures and congregational cultures, in order to have some tools for imagining how, in new circumstances, the founding congregation's deep story might continue to shape the institutional deep story. In these reflections, there is a deep affinity between the notion of deep story and the notion of culture.

I will state the conclusion up front. A sponsoring community's deep story will have to be embedded in lay communities. There will have to be lay appropriations of the congregation's deep story. It takes a long time for a deep story to be lodged in the heart of a community, lodged so deeply that members have no choice but to enact it. The Rite of Christian Initiation for Adults offers a possible model for adult community formation. Religious congregations may have to give up control of the deep story so that it can be developed in a thoroughgoing and coequal lay setting.

The backdrop for these reflections is a model for understanding culture, applicable to both the culture of sponsored institutions and the culture of a congregation's deep story. And the model includes interplay between congregational culture and institutional culture which is not always consciously perceived.

The Culture of the Founding Charism

The Association of Catholic Colleges and Universities has been addressing the relationship between founding religious congregations and Catholic colleges and universities. I would like to name several related parts of the challenge, and discuss one of them at greater length.

First, it is useful to think of both the founding deep story and the university in terms of institutional culture. It is to this notion of culture that I will return at greater length.

Second, while charismatic religious have always been important to founding efforts, the truth is that the effectiveness of the deep story in large institutions owes more to its advocacy by the institution's component social groups and local communities. Professed religious communities are becoming fewer in number. If the deep story is to continue having a constitutive presence, it will still need to be embedded in social groups, but in most places these will be lay communities. Forming lay communities in which the founding narrative is embedded is a different and more complex socialization process than sharing the story with individual lay persons. Understanding the process in terms of culture suggests strategies.

I will return now to the perspective named above: a cultural model for thinking about the task of sponsoring religious institutions.

A Cultural Model for Thinking about
Charism and Institutions

The ACCU study speaks of an earlier time when the founding deep story was promoted by having religious permeate every sector of the institution—the "permeation" model. We cannot do that with our numbers any longer. But permeating institutional culture remains an ideal. I think that a model for understanding all the layers that support a culture offers a way to think differently about permeating the institution with the founding storied intuitions.

Because a culture is a very complex social reality, it is not just useful but vital to understand its many layers. Each of the five elements named below suggests strategies that deserve individual attention.

Their approach to culture is shaped by a number of people who have studied it in depth. I indebted especially to Clifford Geertz, Stanislas Breton, and Jacob Neusner who have written extensively on the topic, and to my colleague Michael Cowan who has helped me understand the centrality of culture to social analysis. The elements below are not separate and discrete, but intertwined. Any organic process of socialization will entail all of these elements.

Mythos

Every culture has great narratives, often invested with mythic elements: the creation story, Noah and the flood, the three kings, Peter finding a coin in a fish's mouth. The Easter Vigil is a magnificent introduction to the Judeo-Christian mythos. The Hebrew Scriptures are full of mythos: creation, the flood, the day the sun stood still, the birth of Isaac to Sarah and Abraham at ages ninety and one-hundred respectively. Concerning the latter, Frederick Buechner says that Abraham and Sarah "are laughing at the idea of a baby's being born in the geriatric ward and Medicare's picking up the tab" (Buechner, 1977, 50).

Plato said that every great truth must be adumbrated by myth. Mythos captures the imagination and the feelings of a people when a story and/or a person is larger than life. All myths are true. They are not mere stories, but great narratives of the exceptional power.

In her book *Pathways to Re-Creating Religious Communities*, Patricia Wittberg notes, for example, how much attention religious orders tend to give to the special character of their founders and foundresses, and how relatively little attention to the intricate social forces at work in any institution's origins. Many accounts of a community's origins, she says, especially when written by the congregation's own members, "have tended to over-emphasize the individual and supernatural at the expense of the societal" (Wittberg, 1996, 8). This is a form of mythologization. It would be a rare congregation that lacked mythologized narratives. Mythologizing is not something one sits down and decides to do; it is the way human imagination captures fundamental experiential data. But, as Wittberg says, understanding accurately the social matrix of a congregation's origin is also critical, and that fits into the next category.

I am in an institution which has developed its own mythos in the course of a century and a half. This institutional mythos is deeply marked by our congregation's mythos but is not merely identical to it. Our sponsored parishes are like that. We bring our own mythos; but so does a Catholic culture.

Logos

Logos names all the ways in which a culture is analyzed, explained, interpreted, and understood, both intellectually and conceptually. The Declaration of Independence, the new *Catechism of the Catholic Church*, the documents of a religious congregation's general chapter, the Mission Statement of University, a parish, a hospital, or a legal clinic, etc., are all examples of logos at work in a culture.

In periods of great change, social groups tend to produce documents "to recapture the essence." Often the motivation is fear of losing identity. Documents start abounding in times of crisis and deep change, seeking a convincing logos. This book is itself an example.

Pathos

In his book, *Vanquished Nation, Broken Spirit: The Virtues of the Heart in Formative Judaism*, the Jewish scholar Jacob Neusner explores the role of affect in any social construction of reality. "As an individual, I link my deepest personal emotions to the...transcendent faith of the social group of which I am a part" (Neusner, 1987, 4). How we feel about things is as intimately linked to identity as how we think about things. Neusner says that emotions lay down judgment in ways connected with rational cognition. Without the affective impulse, there is no urgency or passion to choose.

Human pathos is intimately linked with our judgments about significance. It is the affective element of any community's life which "tames the heart" (141), but tames it in the sense of making it one's own, appropriating it, bringing it into the fold.

I have been on the faculty of four universities sponsored by different religious congregations. I know how the same word (community, for example, or poverty) can carry different meanings and feelings, and how it can function differently in each setting. There are no elements that are absolutely unique to any religious congregation and its founding charism. But how different elements are "felt" is what gives them their special significance and gives any deep story its particular configuration. This pathos component of the social construction of reality rarely gets explicit attention.

Symbolos

Every culture has rituals and symbols that encode and pass on identity. The liturgical calendar is one example. Perhaps nothing so defines Catholic culture as Eucharist.

In national culture, national holidays ritualize a country's self-understanding: through the use of symbols pilgrim costumes at Thanksgiving; paper hatchets and pictures of a cherry tree, or a shovel and a piece of coal with which to write on the shovel on Presidents' Day; the song "We Shall Overcome" on Martin Luther King Day. Probably all religious communities have injected ritual from their traditions into sponsored institutions. Keeping these rituals alive, and also in touch with their origins, is an effective part of guaranteeing that the power of the founding narrative shall continue. Rituals and symbols are probably the key places where pathos is encoded, and essential passions are evoked and nurtured.

Ethos

In Europe you hold your knife with your right hand, you cut the meat speared by the fork in your left hand. Then you introduce the just cut piece of meat into your mouth with your left hand. In the US you put your knife down, transfer your fork to your right hand, then re-spear the meat and eat it with your right hand. Whether or not you observe proper table etiquette depends on what you do and where you do it. In Morocco you might just eat with your fingers and pieces of bread.

How does someone comport him or her self? Sometimes when we

say someone "just doesn't get it," we are identifying some ethos that is out of kilter. My father used to say sometimes, "We just don't do that in this house." People of good will may be put off by the style in one congregation, yet fit exceedingly well in another.

Comportment is a helpful word. How do people comport themselves with respect to each other, to visitors, to the world beyond the community residence? These are most often not moral issues, but matters of style that define a culture. The French philosopher Maurice Merleau-Ponty held that comportment (or behavior) is itself a quite primordial way of thinking.

Members of religious communities who visit other religious communities easily recognize that "it's different there," without being able easily to put their finger on the explicit differences. Not better. Not worse. Just different.

Style is another kind of gloss on ethos, another way of talking about comportment. Marianist style is different than Franciscan, Mercy, St. Joseph, Dominican, Jesuit, Sacred Heart, Oblate, or Benedictine style. Western style is different than Asian style. Explicit morality is a key element of ethos (transmitted with the support of logos, symbolos, and mythos), but certainly does not exhaust ethos. Ethos is about behavioral expectations in any culture, and it does not mean that all the expectations are praiseworthy. The dark side of any deep story also has a style. Most importantly, style is full of gifts.

How a university describes rank and tenure requirements for example, is a clue to ethos, like other regulations in an institution's faculty handbook. The requirements for promotion are clear in most institutions—sometimes they are written down and sometimes folks who have been there a while "just know." I have been a faculty member in graduate pastoral ministry programs for a long while. In the Association of Graduate Programs in Ministry, we have examined numerous programs. Program descriptions do not vary greatly. But the cultures in which they function do vary greatly, and so does the ministerial style of graduates from various institutions. There is some parallel here with how differently novitiate and formation programs shape candidates into the style of the community.

The impact of a founding charism on "style" is another reflection of ethos, of how one comports oneself in the world.

All congregations have examination procedures to admit candidates to perpetual profession. Sometimes the judgments that I have heard, pro or con, are hard to reconcile with observed behaviors, but the instincts about whether someone "fits" or not are usually quite accurate, and people give the best "reasons" they can for their instinct about it all. The ethos is not necessarily a moral question, although it can be. But somehow we just seem to know when someone gets it, or just doesn't get it.

Deep Storied Lay Communities

I remember an article some years back by a college student who said that he was tired of hearing that "the church needs you." It may be true, he said, but he heard precious little about what the Good News of Jesus Christ had in store for him. Why should young people be interested in the gospel in the first place? How does it redeem their young experience? What difference can it really make? How would their relationship with God and with each other be better off with church than without it?

Why, similarly, is close association with the spirituality of a religious congregation, good not just for us who need help, but good for lay women and men whether we need them or not to continue our apostolic commitments? There is a parallel with lay ministry. Why is lay ministry a right thing to do, not because there is a shortage of priests, but because it fits the character of the people of God?

The life of the church has been enriched over so many centuries by the spiritualities of religious orders. There have often been third orders and associations of different kinds. It is not that we are beginning to do an entirely new thing. What may be new is breaking dependence upon the congregations. What may also be new is promoting a lay appropriation of the deep story, turning it loose for some new creative increment. Ministry is now being developed in those ways through lay appropriations of its character and functions. What may also be new is the formation not just of individuals, but of lay communities who live from a thoroughly lay appropriation of the founding narrative.

Community life has been essential to active, apostolic religious congregations. The laity who are able to assume responsibility for the continuation of effective sponsorship of institutions will have to be in community because the logic of their spirituality requires it, not just to fill in for the absence or paucity of professed religious.

In my Marianist tradition, there has long been a great collaborative ease between religious and laity, but until recently the legitimate autonomy of lay Marianists was hardly recognized by either laity or professed. But in the last dozen years there have been three gatherings of lay Marianists internationally: first in Santiago, Chile (1993); then in Lliria, Spain (1997); and most recently in Philadelphia (2001). They produced documents first on their identity, then on their mission, and then on the communal character of lay Marianist identity. In these documents one can recognize Marianist mythos, symbolos, logos, pathos, and ethos, but they have a different look from those in which professed Marianists announce themselves.

Lay communities promoted by Fr. William Joseph Chaminade and Adele de Batz de Tranquelleon were established in Bordeaux beginning in 1800. In 1816 the Marianist woman's order was founded, and in 1817 the men's order, and the lay communities continued though they later lost their sense of an autonomous, interdependent identity. What I am proposing is not a mere recovery, but a true re-creation, a reinvention of the meaning of Marianist laity, because the times demand it—because there is a beating of great wings.

Programmatic Thinking to Promote Effective Socialization

Taking into programmatic consideration the five elements named above, we might then consider different levels or degrees of socialization, depending upon people's interests and commitment. In each case, there should be elements of mythos, symbolos, logos, pathos, and ethos. The following programmatic list is for an academic institution.

Basics for everyone. What should everyone be continually exposed to at the most basic level, e.g., orientation classes for students, parents or spouses of students, orientation for Board members, administrators, faculty, contributors; formats for job applications and search processes; mission statements; strategic planning; etc?

Intermediates for some. What might some middle level socialization look like for people genuinely curious and interested? What would some further exposure to Catholic and congregational culture look like (e.g., some very attractive elective courses, some public lectures, some retreat days; and recourse to Catholic and congregational culture in the formulation of a core curriculum)?

Fuller integration. What forms would strong, personal commitment take? Membership in an active community would be part of this, for the congregational and Catholic deep stories are available to a culture only if they themselves are embedded in smaller social groups within that culture.

Who are the people whose socialization into Catholic and sponsoring charism merits particular attention, always respectful of their interests, background, experience? It is an obvious list:

- board members
- faculty, administrators, and staff
- students and their families, alumni
- the larger communities external to this institution.

The list would be different in others kinds of institutions. We might, for example, name doctors, nurses, laboratory staff, and so on for a health center.

An Organic Process

As complex as all of this may sound, those of us with real interest in the enduring presence of Catholic and Marianist identity could profitably pay attention to each of the five cultural features described briefly above. The purpose of a paradigm derived from experience is to elucidate the meaning of the present, and the shaping of experience in the future. We do not have to talk about "deep story" and "charism" and "institutional culture" in these ways. But it would be to our advantage to understand well the dynamics of cultural socialization and reflect them in our planning and implementation. The five items cannot just be applied mechanically to a planning process, but serious planning, to be effective, will have to reflect in some way or another this cultural complexity.

FOR DISCUSSION

1. The cultural model proposed looks at five dimensions of any culture. For each of the five, name some cultural characteristics of your congregation's deep story.

Mythos

Logos

Pathos

Symbolos

Ethos

2. Socialization in a deep story is a long, intricate process. Does your community support the development of lay associates? If so, how does a lay appropriation of the deep story both resemble and differ from the religious life appropriation of the same deep story?

NINE

EPILOGUE:
COMMUNITY AS PROPHET

The sense of mission is at the very heart of every form of consecrated life. To the extent that consecrated persons live a life completely devoted to the Father, held fast by Christ, and animated by the Spirit, they cooperate effectively in the mission of the Lord Jesus and contribute in a particularly profound way to the renewal of the world. (*Vita consecrata*, #25)

The consecrated life has the prophetic task of recalling and serving the divine plan for humanity as it is announced in Scripture and as it emerges from an attentive reading of the signs of God's providential action in history. (*Vita consecrata*, #73)

Taking the Prophetic Leap

Most active, apostolic congregations are doing very good work, and are meeting real needs in solid Church work. But the Nygren/Ukeritis research showed that the issue for the future of religious life is not whether we are doing good work, but whether we are responding to critical, unmet human needs in ways that are shaped by our deep story, and driven by our relationship with God. The fact that most of us are doing good work and meeting real needs is what often makes it very difficult to name needs that are more critical and require significant personal and institutional conversion.

There are two kinds of issues that hold us back. In her discussion of what might invite "virtuosi" Catholics to consider religious life, Patricia Wittberg observes

> ...that the life calling of all types of virtuosi is to formulate a response to "the sharpest anguish" or the "sustained dissatisfaction" of society and culture...[and] their success will depend on whether or not they can [actually] uncover the "sharpest anguish" of the twenty-first century, and on how effectively they can formulate a spiritual answer to it. (Wittberg, 1996, 61, 62)

We cannot simply abandon all maintenance commitments and ride white horses into the prophetic arena. We have many serious current responsibilities. On the other hand, current responsibilities can paralyze us. That is often the issue that holds us back. We have fewer young people who push hard for the prophetic. The young are not the only ones who push for the prophetic, but there is something to be said for the energy of youth.

The second obstacle to embracing prophetic explorations is that we always want the entire congregation to move together so that no one is left behind. Wittberg observes rightly that this is not possible. Developing a new vision with sufficient strength to refound will inevitably leave some behind (Wittberg, 1995, 92). We have to accept that. If it works, many will come along later.

The Prophet and the Pain of the World

Abraham Heschel's two-volume study of the prophets describes prophecy and its origins as our sympathetic entry into the pathos of God. (In all the Heschel citations that follow, I have injected inclusive language.) Heschel is interested in clues to the consciousness of prophets—what the "insides" of prophetic life look and feel like.

He begins with what it is like to encounter a prophet. "The situation of a person immersed in the prophet's words is one of being exposed to a ceaseless shattering of indifference, and one needs a skull of stone to remain callous to such blows" (Heschel, I, 1962, xii). That is why the prophet is rarely a popular figure. It is immersion in the pain of the world and in the pain of God that gives prophets their authority. The pain of founders and foundresses is legendary.

"Prophecy," Heschel writes, "is the voice that God has lent to the silent poor, a voice to the plundered poor, a crossing point of God and the human person. It is a form of living, a crossing point of God and humanity." We do not become the voice of the silent poor through a conceptual understanding of poverty, but through immediate contact with the lived experience of the poor. This comment must be contextualized without watering it down. If everyone spent all their time and energy addressing immediate needs, the dysfunctional systems responsible for them would be empowered to continue, since everyone would only be picking up the pieces.

There is a necessary rhythm between mercy needs and justice needs. In my congregation, the Brothers who are in India, Mexico, Korea, and East Africa bring into our common pool of resources the experience and the character of destitution. How we listen to them is critical. If we listen to them, see pictures, and read the right materials, we easily feel compassion and sometimes a just anger. But it is more redemptive to listen to their pathos about the poor, so that we feel their feelings about the issue, we feel their pain and frustration, we feel their fierceness.

By fierceness, I do not mean aggressiveness. I mean resolve, a relentlessness when relenting is not an moral option. In his book on small groups, *Sharing the Journey*, Robert Wuthnow says that four out of every ten Americans now belong to some sort of small group, most often ones that have many characteristics of a support group. Such groups are gathered, but rarely sent by concerns outside the group. Wuthnow says that support groups, which value understanding and tolerance, often make God into a member of the support group.

There is a danger if God becomes a being with the same characteristics as those experienced in one's support group.... Spirituality is domesticated....Sacredness ceases to be the mysterium tremendum that commands awe and reverence....God becomes a source of advice and comfort...calming our anxieties rather than moving mountains....But a domesticated view of the sacred has always been worrisome to the saints and the sages who have struggled most deeply with its meaning and implication. (Wuthnow, 1994, 231, 255)

In brief, not simply direct immersion into the experience of poverty, but feeling the feelings of those who are so immersed, will prevent us from domesticating God and losing God's fierceness when it comes to injustice.

These remarks reflect the tensions that many of us feel in religious life, because most of us come from middle-class backgrounds, in a culture that often tends to say that religion is a private matter and does not belong in politics—unaware that both Aristotle and Thomas Aquinas consider politics a virtue, for it is how systems are managed and transformed. The only way, in fact. Not only are most of us middle class, but we are well educated as well, and this can be decisive for the work of social justice. Heschel writes:

Perhaps the prophet knew more about the secret obscenity of sheer unfairness, about the unnoticed malignancy of established patterns of indifference, than those whose knowledge depends solely on intelligence and observation....The prophet's ear perceives the silent sigh (Heschel I, 1962, 9).

We do not want our understanding of critical, unmet human need to rest solely on intelligence and observation. If we are not in the field, we want to understand through the understanding of others, and especially through their feelings about human misery. We can see the world through their point of view "for the prophets see the world from the point of view of God" (Heschel I, 1962, 14). But our education can contribute in important ways to the transformation of society through developed skills in social analysis, an understanding of the function of change agents, a solid grasp of our deep stories, sensibilities created by Catholic tradition, and our openness to the power of the Spirit. Whenever through education we can help sensitize the middle class to social justice issues, we develop a power base for significant social change.

The Prophet and God

In the world of biblical prophets, God is intimately affected by all that occurs in the world he has made. Heschel calls the pathos of God a "living care...no mere contemplative survey of the world but a passionate summons" (Heschel II, 1962, 4).

The prophet is one who, because of his deeply personal relationship with God, is able to share God's feelings, God's pathos, God's concern for human history. But it is not just individuals, but also communities that can have a prayer life that reflects a profoundly interpersonal relationship with God—communities can feel the pathos of God and get to that point only by community prayer, by community love for Scripture, by community engagement in social action aimed at remaking God's world and above all intuiting God's pathos (loving care) about it. To "feel with" is exactly what the two Greek words mean that make up the word sym[with]pathy[feeling].

> This moving awareness of God's care and sorrows concerning the world, the prophet's communion with the divine in experience and suffering, is of such evident and striking power and authority, evincing such complete surrender and devotion, that it may offer a basic understanding of religious existence.... The depth of the soul becomes the point where an understanding for God and a harmony with transcendent possibility spring to birth. (Heschel II, 1962, 91)

The point of Heschel's understanding of prophecy is that while the prophet is personally incensed at injustice, that is not the fundamental driving force behind his message. It is the prophet's profound relationship with God that allows him to feel God's righteous anger, and then to clothe her/his experience of injustice in the world with the pain of God.

The verb "to feel" has a variety of meanings in English, not all of them particularly useful in explicating what it means to share in the feelings of God. Some of the meanings that don't apply to prophetic sympathy are "I don't feel good, I have a headache," or "I don't feel like going out today," or "I don't feel comfortable in this apartment." The kinds of feeling that come closer are "I don't like the way our city is addressing homelessness," or "I feel that capital punishment is immoral," or "I feel that the proposed tax structure will alleviate some poverty and I like it." These are feelings that have to do with what kind of a world we choose to help make together. When Heschel talks about how a prophet feels the feelings of God, he means the pathos of God for the shape of human existence, the pathos of God when his children are victimized, or even the pathos of God when we act justly, love tenderly, and walk humbly with God.

In Hebrew anthropology, the seat of personhood is the heart, in contrast to Greek anthropology in which the seat of personhood is the rational mind. The subtitle of Jacob Neusner's *Vanquished Nation, Broken Spirit*, is "The Virtues of the Heart in Formative Judaism." Neusner follows Robert Solomon in understanding the vital role that emotions play in any community's larger social construction. In his description of formative Judaism, Neusner says that "the power of emotions harnessed to the forces of history" is his concern (Neusner, 1987, 14). He holds that emotion, which he sees as a system of judgments, is what links the personal and private with the social and public (ibid.).

Every congregation has a characteristic "mood" or "style" or "instinctive manner" or, better yet, "feeling texture." Each congregation has its own nexus of formative emotions, and they are an integral part of a community's deep story. What Neusner says about individual members of a nation applies, *mutatis mutandis*, to how new members of religious congregations are formed over time.

> ...individuals, seeing themselves as private individuals, were taught to feel for themselves all of those emotions in which, in the way of life and world view of the larger society, the system as a whole gave full expression. In consequence, how individuals felt in their hearts, their virtuous attitudes, turned out to correspond exactly to how the nation lived as a whole, in its politics and social culture. (Neusner, 1988, 18-19)

Formation does not merely instill in us historical data and congregational ideas; rather, it forms how we experience the world, how we "feel" the world. It is the "bias" out of which we experience, the perspective that makes experience possible. Formative notions and formative emotions co-construct this bias. We have to stand somewhere in the world, and see it from where we stand, and that is a bias. Throughout these reflections, I have spoken about a community's deep story. Our deep stories are our bias, and within them is shaped our congregation's fundamental pathos, our essential passions.

One way to describe the genius of foundresses and founders is to say that they knew the pain of the world and experienced the pathos of God towards it. But no one experiences all the pain of the world. Those who founded our communities belonged to particular moments in history and felt needs that were proximate, pressing, and unaddressed. Most of our founding prophets had favorite passages from Scripture, favorite pieces of the tradition, favorite spirited geniuses. One could say that it was those particular influences on their personal prayer and their passionate relationships with God that led them into the pathos of God—God, who had already come as self-gift into their committed lives.

And God came to founders and foundresses as God always comes, historically mediated. "Reading" God and "reading" the world are not interchangeable, but neither are they separable. That's the beginning of a new deep story and a transmittable pathos. Significant others must validate the deep story with commitment before it begins to look like charism in the world. When that happens, a new religious social culture is in the making. Prophecy is not what we do with our ultimate issues, but how we respond to what concerns *God* ultimately.

Courage

It is easier to write about addressing critical human needs than to actually do something about meeting them. If no one is meeting a need, then striving to meet it is counter-cultural to the core. Going against the stream is a metaphor for counter-cultural comportment.

The word "courage" comes from French, and is related to the word for heart, *coeur*. The French dictionary on my desk renders the expression *avoir du coeur* of "having courage," "to have heart." At its root, courage is a profoundly affective gift: people moved to the core (also a heart word) at the plight of other people. When Samuel is confused by God's choice of David, Yahweh tells him not to judge by human wisdom: "God does not see as human beings see; they look at appearances, but YHWH looks at the heart" (1 Sam 16:7).

In an earlier work I traced the role of heart in Hebrew anthropology:

> Heart is where what I ultimately stand for resides, and is consequently where *who* I am is defined. I may say things that are discordant with my heart and do things that are unfaithful to my heart, but if my heart is in the right place I am capable of remorse. Heart is not emotion in the more ordinary sense of the word, though that is included. Heart refers to the valuational structure whence flow the loves and hates that define me. It is not the fluctuating emotions of the hour that yield my character, but the abiding sense of where preciousness lies for me. (Lee, 1993, 67-68)

Jacob Neusner has tried to describe how a people, a social group can have a heart. The courage of a congregation is a reality, as much as that of its individual members. A great-hearted community stands a solid chance of having (forming) great-hearted individual members.

I have often stressed in this book the role of social analysis, which can focus our attention and understanding upon real situations. That is necessary but insufficient for prophecy. Finally, it is the heart that moves us. And what Heschel is telling us is that when we move, it is not merely our outraged feeling for an unjust situation, as critical as that is, but our feelings of God's outrage, from which prophetic courage is born.

The Social Unit as Prophet

Towards the end of the last of The Four Quartets T.S. Eliot writes:

> We shall not cease from exploration
> And the end of all our exploring
> Will be to arrive where we started
> And know the place for the first time.

We began with a strong hope that there is for religious life a beating of great wings. That was a starting point. God was over his new creation like a bird brooding over its young. The Spirit came at Jesus' baptism in the likeness of a dove.

What interests me more and more with respect to religious life derives from an increased biblical awareness that not only do individuals have their individual experience of God, but that God has a presence to a people in their togetherness as a community. Or, from the other direction, a community has a shared experience of God which is more than the sum total of and different from the experience of God of all individual members.

When all of the things that Abraham Heschel says about the individual prophet are applied to a prophetic community, the question that emerges with urgency is "how does a community as a community feel the feelings of God, the pathos of God, and then assimilate God's pathos into that of the community?" What kind of life of common prayer enables those who gather regularly to feel the feelings of God together? What forms of common life (meals, education, relaxation, etc.) promote a truly communal experience? If we looked at the weekly timetable of several communities, some of whom address this challenge well, what might be the tip off to those who manage this radically communal spirituality?

One thing for sure is that a communal spirituality is no replacement for an individual community member's spirituality. So a related question is: what kind of personal spirituality nourishes and is nourished by a people's God experience?

Where have all the "virtuosi" gone?

I believe that Patricia Wittberg is correct in her view that for a very long time, prior to the Second Vatican Council, religious life and priesthood were the vocational places towards which many virtuosi Catholics were attracted. Part of the "magic" was that these ways of life were popularly called "ways of perfection," suggesting that other "ways" were of lesser quality. That perception was interrupted by the growing recognition that all people are called to the same perfection, and that both married life and single life can, like religious life, be examples of perfection.

Today's Catholic virtuosi have other options. There are more than twice as many lay women and men in various graduate programs in theology in the US Catholic Church than there are seminarians in graduate theology preparing for ordination. These lay women and men are preparing for ministry. There are now more lay people in professional parish ministry (half-time or more) than there are active diocesan priests in parish ministry, and over eighty percent of them are women.

Another option for Catholic virtuosi is the small Christian community, which number between 40,000 and 50,000 in the US Catholic Church today. These Catholics are far more active in church life than the general Catholic population. They do more than any ordinary parish either expects or invites, because they are people who want to do more.

Like all members of religious congregations, I want my order to survive. It is where I have pitched my tent and where I found abundant meaning in my life. But that is not the best reason for wanting religious life to survive, it is not a wrong reason but an insufficient reason. A better reason for wanting religious orders to continue in existence is that the work of God, mediated by the church, needs their prophetic impulse, vision, energy, holiness, and resources.

Throughout this book I have dwelt on three themes and I will conclude with a summary of each.

1. A Relentlessly Dialogic Matrix

What has caused new orders to spring up and old orders to become new orders once again is the relentless dialogue between God's speech to us (especially as mediated by Scripture), the most pressing needs of the world, and a community's deep story (whether a new one in the making or an older one reinvented).

Formation programs must, therefore, respond to the importance of:

1. education in Scripture and theology;

2. education in social analysis and related disciplines; and

3. education in the historically conditioned knowledge of one's own congregation.

2. Collaboration with God in Mission

In the social construction of the reality of active, apostolic religious life, I have suggested that being in permanent mission in the world is a defining hermeneutical perspective for understanding and living celibacy, poverty, and obedience. Each of these sworn commitments supports a common life committed to realizing God's reign in human history.

I have proposed an underlying anthropology that does not make action secondary to contemplation. Action (not activity) describes the human condition; and human action that joins with God's action is nothing short of union with God. In a Teilhardian sense, any improvement we can make in the world and in ourselves is a deeper sacramentalization of Christ in the universe. In this take on religious life, reflective action is an alternative to *contemplare et tradere*.

3. Book, Bread, and Cup

A move from one city to another or even one house to another is a clearing-out time: deciding what to keep and what to leave or toss. Religious life has a long, splendid history. It has had many "houses." But this is moving time. Our language makes this clear: pre-conciliar and post-conciliar; modern and postmodern, second millennium and third millennium, the Enlightenment, and deconstruction.

One form of "cleaning out" applies to our religious practices, the rhythms and contents of our ritual life, putting Word and Eucharist at the absolute center, and choosing carefully from among the many options that will maintain the efficacy of our deep stories.

We all wish it were as easy as rewriting the daily and week time schedules. The most pressing challenge in the restoration of body, bread, and cup to an unmistakable centrality is the recovery of common life. The dialogue between Word and world needs a community with shared history, a willingly embraced accountability, and mutual complicity in mission.

We are indeed counter-culture when, in a culture in which individualism is as strong as ours, we manage to recover a true common life. But that is what the body of Christ is truly like. It's ontological not voluntary. It is what the early Christians called *koinonia*, a Greek word for community from a root meaning "participation." There is the fear in us that we will get lost in the crowd. Catherine LaCugna addressed this fear in her discussion of God with us:

> Koinonia does not swallow up the individual, nor obscure his or her uniqueness and unique contribution, nor take away individual freedom by assimilating it in a collective will. (LaCugna, 1992, 299)

Word and Eucharist must be central in community life, but equally important are the inward conversions that those in religious life must undergo. Only in this way will *koinonia* become a reality for those who gather for body, bread, and cup in parishes across the country.

How body, bread, and cup ground and encourage prophecy has a lot to do with whether Catholic virtuosi feel called to religious life, not because we need them but because the reign of God needs us. But it is possible. Do you not already hear the beating of great wings?

For Discussion

1. Abraham Heschel says that the passion of a prophet is driven by feeling the world with the same feelings with which God feels the world. Perhaps the most crucial question of all is this: how do we get close enough to God to feel God's feelings, as individuals, and especially as a congregation? In our traditions we speak about asceticism, about religious practices, about spiritual exercises, etc. What might those look like?

2. In an article in *Review for Religious*, Elizabeth Dreyer talks about courage as essential if a religious community is to be prophetic (Dreyer, 2003). Courage does not just happen in a particular context if there has not been a pattern of courageous living. A religious order that habitually lives with courage is more likely to bring forth individual courageous religious. What does courage look like as a community lifestyle?

3. What are some modes of communal discernment of both God and world that might give us our best chance at being open to a prophetic existence?

BIBLIOGRAPHY

Documents

Evangelica Testificatio (ET). Apostolic Exhortation of His Holiness Pope Paul VI on the Renewal of the Religious Life According to the Teaching of the Second Vatican Council. June 29, 1971.

Directives for the Mutual Relations between Bishops and Religious in the Church (MR). The Sacred Congregation for Religious and Secular Institutes,and the Sacred Congregation for Bishops. March 14, 1978.

Redemptionis Donum (RD). Apostolic Exhortation of His Holiness Pope John Paul II to Men and Women Religious on their Consecration in the Light of the Mystery of Redemption. March 25, 1984.

Vita Consecrata (VC). Apostolic Exhortation of His Holiness Pope John Paul II on the Consecrated Life. March 25, 1996.

Books and Articles

Arendt, Hannah. *The Human Condition.* Chicago: University of Chicago, 1958.

Bellah, Robert and Richard Madsen, William Sullivan, Ann Swidler, Stephen Tipton. *Habits of the Heart: Individualism and Commitment in American Life.* Berkeley: University of California, 1985.

Berger, Peter. *Sacred Canopy: Elements of a Sociological Theory of Religion.* New York: Doubleday, 1969.

Bihl, Hugh. *The Marianist Presence at the Dawn of the Twenty-first Century.* Madrid: AGSM, 2001.

Boman, Thorlief. *Hebrew Thought Compared with Greek.* Louisville, KY: Westminster John Knox Press, 1960.

Buber, Martin. *I and Thou*. New York: Scribners, 1958.

Buber, Martin, ed. Nahum Glatzer. *The Way of Response*. New York: Schocken, 1996.

Bretall, Robert, ed. *The Empirical Theology of Henry Nelson Wieman*. Carbondale and Edwardsville: Southern Illinois University Press, 1963.

Breton, Stanislas. *The Word and the Cross*. New York: Fordham University Press, 2002.

Brueggemann, Walter. *The Prophetic Imagination*. Minneapolis: Fortress, 1978.

Buechner, Frederick. *Telling the Truth*. San Francisco: Harper & Row, 1977.

Bultmann, Rudolph. *History and Eschatology: The Presence of Eternity*. New York: Harper, 1957.

Chauvet, Louis-Marie. *The Sacraments: The Word of God at the Mercy of the Body*. Collegeville: The Liturgical Press, 2001.

Cooke, Bernard. *The Distancing of God: The Ambiguity of Symbol in History and Theology*. Minneapolis: Fortress, 1990.

Crites, Stephen. "The Narrative Quality of Experience," *Journal of the American Academy of Religion*, (39) 1971.

Crossan, John Dominic. *Jesus*. San Francisco: Harper, 1994.

Dillard, Annie. *Teaching a Stone to Talk*. New York: Harper, 1982.

Dreyer, Elizabeth. "Prophetic Voice in Religious Life," in *Review for Religious* 62/3, 2003.

Erikson, Erik. *Gandhi's Truth: On the Origin of Militant Nonviolence*. New York: W. W. Norton, 1969.

Farley, Edward. *Deep Symbols: Their Postmodern Effacement and Reclamation*. Harrisburg, PA: Trinity Press International, 1996.

Garaudy, Roger. *Marxism in the Twentieth Century*. New York: Scribners, 1970.

Geertz, Clifford. *The Interpretation of Cultures*. New York: Basic Books, 1983.

Hadaway, Kirk, and Penny Marler and Mark Chaves. "What the Polls Don't Show: A Closer Look at U.S. Church Attendance," *American Sociological Review*, 58/6, 1993.

Hanson, Paul. *The People Called: The Growth of Community in the Bible*. San Francisco: HarperCollins, 1986.

Heidegger, Martin, tr. Joan Stambaugh. *Being and Time*. Albany: State University Press of New York, 1996.

Heschel, Abraham. *The Prophets*, volumes. I & II, San Francisco: Harper, 1962.

James, William. *Pragmatism and Other Essays*. New York: Washington Square Press, 1975.

Kelley, John J. *Freedom in the Church: A Documentary History of the Principle of Subsidiary Function*. Dayton: Peter Li, 2000.

Koenig, John. *The Feast of the World's Redemption: Eucharistic Origins and Christian Mission*. Harrisburg, PA: Trinity Press International, 2000.

LaCugna, Catherine. *God for Us: The Trinity and Christian Life*. San Francisco: Harper, 1992.

Lee, Bernard J. "The Appetite of God" in Bernard Lee and Harry Cargas, *Religious Experience and Process Theology: The Pastoral Implications of a Major Modern Movement*. Mahwah, NJ: Paulist Press, 1976.

———. *The Becoming of the Church: A Process Theology of the Structure of Christian Experience*. Mahwah, NJ: Paulist Press, 1974.

———. *The Future Church of 140 BCE: A Hidden Revolution*. New York: Crossroad, 1995.

———. *Jesus and the Metaphors of God: The Christs of the New Testament*. Mahwah, NJ: Paulist Press, 1993.

———. "A Socio-Historical Theology of Charism," in *Review for Religious*, 48/1, Jan-Feb 1989.

Legrand, Hervé-Marie. "The Presidency of the Eucharist According to the Ancient Traditions," in *Worship*, 53/5, September 1979.

Lohfink, Gerhard. *Jesus and Community*. Minneapolis: Fortress, 1984.

Loomer, Bernard M. "S-I-Z-E Is the Measure," in Harry Cargas and Bernard Lee, *Religious Experience and Process Theology: The Pastoral Implications of a Major Modern Movement*. Mahwah, NJ: Paulist Press, 1976.

Macmurray, John. *The Self as Agent*. Atlantic Highlands, NJ: Humanities International Press, 1978.

———. *Persons in Relation*. Amherst, NY: Humanity Books, 1999.

Macy, Gary. *The Banquet's Kingdom: A Short History of the Theologies of the Lord's Supper*. Mahwah, NJ: Paulist Press, 1992.

Metz, Johannes. *Followers of Christ: Perspectives on the Religious Life*. Mahwah, NJ: Paulist Press, 1978.

Mitchell, Nathan. *Cult and Controversy: The Worship of Eucharist Outside Mass*. New York: Pueblo, 1982.

Neusner, Jacob. *Vanquished Nation, Broken Spirit: The Virtues of the Heart in Formative Judaism*. New York: Cambridge, 1987.

Nye, Naomi Shihan. *Yellow Glove*. Portland: Breitenbusch Books, 1986.

Nygren, David and Miriam Ukeritis. "The Future of Religious Orders in the United States: Executive Summary," *Origins*, 22/15, Sept. 24, 1992.

Osborne, Kenan. *Christian Sacraments in a Postmodern World: A Theology for the Third Millennium*. Mahwah, NJ: Paulist Press, 1999.

Peirce, Charles Sanders, ed. Philip Wiener. *Charles S. Peirce: Selected Writings*. New York: Dover, 1958.

Pontifical Biblical Commission. "Interpretation of the Bible in the Catholic Church," *Origins*, 1993.

Putnam, Robert. *Bowling Alone: The Collapse and Revival of American Community*. New York: Simon & Schuster, 2000.

Rahner, Karl, et al. "Christianity and the Future," in *The Future of Man and Christianity*. Chicago: Argus Communications, 1969.

Rahner, Karl. *Hearer of the Word*. New York: Continuum, 1994.

Renfro, Jean Marie. "Religious Charism: Definition, Rediscovery and Implications," in *Review for Religious*, 45/4, 1986.

Rilke, Rainer Maria, tr. J. B. Leishman. *Possibility of Being: A Collection of Poems*. New York: New Directions, 1977.

Roof, Wade Clark. *Spiritual Marketplace: Baby Boomers and the Remaking of American Religion*. Princeton: Princeton University Press, 1999.

Schneiders, Sandra. *Finding the Treasure: Locating Catholic Religious Life in a New Ecclesial and Cultural Context*. Mahwah, NJ: Paulist Press, 2000.

———. *Selling All: Commitment, Consecrated Celibacy, and Community in Catholic Religious Life*. Mahwah, NJ: Paulist Press, 2001.

Schillebeeckx, Edward. *The Eucharist*. London: Sheed & Ward, 1968.

Schama, Simon. *Citizens: A Chronicle of the French Revolution*. New York: Random House Vintage, 1989.

Tracy, David. *The Analogical Imagination: Christian Theology and the Culture of Pluralism*. New York: Crossroad, 1981.

Turner, Victor. *The Ritual Process: Structure and Anti-Structure*. Ithaca: Cornell University Press, 1977.

Weber, Max. H. H. Gerth and C. Wright Mills, eds. *From Max Weber: Essays in Sociology*. New York: Oxford University Press, 1958.

Weber, Max. *The Sociology of Religion*. Boston: Beacon Press, 1964.

———. *The Theory of Social and Economic Organization*. New York: Free Press, 1947.

West, Gerald. *Biblical Hermeneutics: Modes of Reading the Bible in the South African Context*. Maryknoll, NY: Orbis Books, 1995.

Whitehead, Alfred North. *Process and Reality*, corrected edition. New York: The Free Press, 1978.

———. *Science and the Modern World*. New York: Macmillan, 1925.

Whitehead, Evelyn Eaton, and James D. Whitehead. *Community of Faith: Crafting Christian Communities Today*. Mystic, CT: Twenty-Third Publications, 1992.

Wieman, Henry Nelson. *The Source of Human Good*. Carbondale Edwardsville: Southern Illinois University Press, 1946.

Wittberg, Patricia. *Pathway to Re-creating Religious Communities.* Mahwah, NJ: Paulist Press, 1996.

Worsley, Peter. *The Trumpet Shall Sound: A Study of "Cargo" Cults in Melanasia.* New York: Schocken, 1968.

Wright, Eugene. *Erikson: Religion and Identity.* New York: Seabury, 1982.

Wuthnow, Robert. *Sharing the Journey: Support Groups and America's New Quest for Community.* New York: The Free Press, 1994.